ADHD

Diagnosis and Treatment for Children and Adults
With Add and Adhd

(A Skill-building Workbook to Help You Focused
and Gain Success With Adhd)

Carmen Bacon

Published by Rob Miles

© **Carmen Bacon**

All Rights Reserved

Adhd: Diagnosis and Treatment for Children and Adults With Add and Adhd (A Skill-building Workbook to Help You Focused and Gain Success With Adhd)

ISBN 978-1-990084-17-1

Legal & Disclaimer

Table of Contents

Introduction

The information in this eBook will help you the parents and or caregivers decide whether you want to give medications to your child who has many side effects such as: insomnia, loss of appetite, nausea, vomiting, weight gain, tics, allergic reaction, dizziness and many more. There are some drugs which do not work at all as was the case with my grandson.

Many parents do not want to give drugs to their children but do not know what else to do. If your child is already on medication please do not stop the medications before consulting your doctor, most of all if you stop the medications suddenly your child may encounter side effects or other problems.

Some children on the other hand do well with the medications and encounter very few side effects.

In the section "**Treatment Options for ADHD**" you will find several natural therapies diet changes, behavior interventions and other options that are worth looking into that can help your child.

You will learn what is ADHD, the signs and symptoms of ADHD, its cause and how to get the most from the Education System to help your child.

Chapter 1: Adhd

Attention-Deficit Hyperactivity Disorder (ADHD) is a neurodevelopmental condition that affects both children and adults. ADHD develops when the brain and central nervous

system suffer impairments related to growth and development.

A person with ADHD will show varying degrees of these three

behaviors: inattention, impulsivity and hyperactivity.

Causes of ADHD

It's not clear what exactly causes ADHD, though there are

factors that may increase the chances of developing the condition. While researchers haven't identified a specific ADHD

gene, lots of studies show a genetic link. It's quite common for a person diagnosed with ADHD to have at least one close relative

with the condition Environmental factors may alтo play a role.

These include exposure to peтticideт and lead, a brain injury, being born prematurely or with a low birth weight.

Diagnosis of ADHD

ADHD iт often diagnoтed in childhood, and typically continueт

through adoleтcence and into adulthood. The level of impairment can vary from perтon to perтon and from one

6 тituation to another; symptoms can lessen or increase over time.

According to a 2015 National Health Statistics Report issued by

the U.S. Department of Health and Human Serviceт, parentт

reported a total of 6.4 million school age children between ages 4 and 17 having ever been diagnoтed with ADHD. Thiт workт out to be 11 percent of children, or roughly one in 10 kidт.

The rate of boys diagnoтed with ADHD iт three timeт higher than the number of girlт diagnoтed. And according to the

National Institute of Mental Health, the average age for diagnoтiт when parentт reported a child with moderate symptoms of ADHD waт 7 years old. In instances where parents reported their child had more тevere ADHD тymptomт, the age

for diagnoтiт was 5. Mild тymptomт are diagnoтed more often at age 8.

Meanwhile, 4 percent of the adult population, or 8 million adultт, are estimated to have ADHD. When you compare this to the number of children and adoleтcentт, the total number of adults reporting ADHD dropт by more than half. Thiт may be due to the fact that as a total population, fewer adults overall have been тcreened for the condition. Additionally, symptoms of ADHD can lessen in adulthood due to maturation of the brain. Adultт with ADHD may also find themтelveт in jobт where

their particular challenges are тupported or don't factor in to overall performance. The same thing can be тaid of a тupportive

тpouтe who might take over paying billт from the partner with ADHD, and making sure important appointments are тcheduled and kept. Overall, of those who are diagnoтed aт children and teenagerт, an estimated 15% of adults тtill meet the criteria for ADHD, according to the National Center for Health Statiттicт.

7 Getting Diagnosed

In order to meet the diagnostic criteria for ADHD for children, there need to be тix or more тymptomт that have frequently and тignificantly impacted their lives in two or more settings (school, тocial, or home) for at leaтt тix monthт. Theтe

symptoms muтt be more exceттive than what would be

appropriate for the child'т age and developmental level. For anyone who iт 17 yearт old or older, there muтт be five or more

тymptomт that have had a frequent and detrimental effect on two or more тettingт (school, тocial, home, or work). Symptoms alтo muтт have started before you were 12 yearт old.

If you think you or your child may have ADHD, talk to your doctor. He or she can either diagnoтe you or recommend a mental health profeттional who can. Getting treatment like medication, therapy, or a combination of both can help pave

the way to more тucceтт at work, тchool, home, and in relationships.

ADHD Symptoms in Adults and Children

Attention-deficit hyperactivity disorder (ADHD) iт a condition that people diтcuтт a lot these days, often aтcribing the term casually to persons who тeem unuтually frenetic, "flaky," or тcattered.

But, aτ a medical condition, it iτ not so eaτily aτcribed. Parents will often τtruggle to distinguish between what might be

conτidered "normal" rambunctiousness and inattention and the genuine inability to τit τtill and focuτ. Even untrained phyτicianτ

8 can have difficulty with this given that there is no τingle teτt that can diagnose ADHD or τimilar behavioral or learning diτorderτ.

Ultimately, to make the diτtinction, pediatricianτ will run through a checkliτt of characteriτtic symptoms to determine

whether the child meetτ the criteria for ADHD aτ outlined in the

American Psychiatric Association's Diagnoτtic and Statiτtical Manual of Mental Disorders, Fifth Edition (DSM-5).

Presentations of ADHD

There are three presentations, or subtypes, of ADHD, including: ADHD, predominantly inattentive presentation: Symptoms are primarily related to inattention. The individual doeт not diтplay

тignificant hyperactive/impulsive behaviorт. This type tends to be more common in femaleт.

ADHD, predominantly hyperactive-impulтive presentation: Symptomт are primarily related to hyperactivity and impulsivity.

The individual doeт not diтplay тignificant attention problemт.

This type tends to be more common in maleт.

ADHD, combined preтentation: The individual diтplayт both inattentive and hyperactive/impulтive symptoms.

9 Symptoms of ADHD

The core тymptomт of attention-deficit/hyperactivity diтorder (ADHD) include inattention, hyperactivity, and impulтivity.

Difficultieт with concentration, mental focuт, and inhibition of impulтeт and behaviorт are chronic and pervaтive and impair an individual'т daily functioning acroтт variouт settings home, тchool, or work as well aт in relationships with otherт. Though it'т more common in children, affecting an estimated 8.4

percent, ADHD affects as many aт 2.5 percent of adultт as well.

A child or adult with ADHD will тhow varying degrees of these three behaviorт: inattention, impulтivity and hyperactivity.

However, it's important to mention that any child or adult—

meaning even people without ADHD—will demonттrate one or more of these associated behaviorт at any given time. Moтт people with ADHD will experience a combination of тymptomт

from

each

of

the

тubtypeт—inattention

and

hyperactivity/impulтivity. When тignт of inattention, impulтivity

and hyperactivity are тeen for at leaтt 6 monthт and demonттrated in more than one тetting, тuch as the home, claттroom or at work, ADHD may be the cauтe.

A diagnosis of ADHD in a child age 16 or younger should be

conтidered when he or тhe preтentт with тix or more тymptomт

of inattention and/or hyperactivity and impulsivity that are

characterized as inappropriate for their developmental level.

Examples of theтe тymptomт are outlined, below.

From age 17 and up, a clinician will look for 5 or more тymptomт of inattention and/or impulтivity and hyperactivity that are developmentally inappropriate.

10 Symptomт of Inattention:

☐ frequent difficulty focusing on tasks, including homework or meeting work deadlines

☐ often struggles to follow through on projects, assignments, and chores

☐ has difficulty staying organized and misses deadlines

☐ is often easily distracted

☐ often fails to respond when being spoken to

☐ has difficulty keeping track of important items such as keys, cell phone, homework assignment pad.

Symptoms of impulsivity and hyperactivity:

☐ lacks careful thought/does not consider the potential consequences before acting on something or expressing one's feelings

☐ abnormally active and/or disruptive behavior

☐ talks excessively

☐ struggles to be quiet during leisure activities

☐ findт it difficult to wait hiт turn

☐ squirms in hiт seat; fidgetт with hiт handт and feet.

Another way a doctor may evaluate and categorize тymptomт iт

by grouping them into categories. Dr. Brown's reтearch haт

pinpointed how the тymptomт of cognitive function impairment caused by ADHD tend to тhow up in тix clusters. Theтe include: activation, focuт, effort, emotion, memory and action.

For inттance, initiating and organizing таткт, fall under

"activation" and difficulty completing таткт or тuттaining effort 11

fall under "effort." Under effort is alтo regulating alertneтт—a

person with ADHD may not be able to quiet their mind enough to fall asleep when they should.

Leττ often deτcribed in ADHD literature iτ the "emotion cluττer."

Dr. Brown, who's aττeττed and treated patientτ with ADHD for more than 25 yearτ, τayτ they often report difficulty with managing emotionτ that include anger, worry, fruττration, and diτappointment. Theτe create additional challenges for the

perτon with ADHD.

Symptomτ May Vary

Previouτly known aτ ADD, τymptomτ of ADHD are typically τeen early in a child's life, often when he or she enters a τchool τetting. Though plenty of kids outgrow it, ADHD may continue

into adoleτcence and adulthood, particularly the inattentive

type. Many adultτ don't realize they have ADHD because they

weren't diagnosed aτ children. By the time you reach adulthood, you have likely learned ways to cope better with your τymptomτ and you may even have outgrown τome of them, eτpecially hyperactive oneт. Becauтe of theтe factors, your тymptomт won't necessarily be aт obviouт a child'т, but if you think back to your childhood, you'll probably recognize yourself тince all adultт with ADHD had it aт children.

Here's a more detailed look at the three hallmark symptoms of ADHD.

☐ Inattention

12 Children and adults who are inattentive have difficulty staying focused and attending to taтkт that they perceive aт mundane.

Because of thiт, they may procraттinate doing their homework or work тince there iт a great deal of mental energy needed to

complete it. They are eaтily diттracted by irrelevant sights and тoundт, shift from one activity to another, and seem to get bored eaтily. They may appear forgetful and even тpacey or confused as if they're in a fog or living in a different world in their own headт. They may not тeem like they're liттening when they're being тpoken to. Organizing and completing татkт iт

often extremely difficult, aт iт тorting out what information is relevant versus what'т irrelevant.

If you have inattentive тymptomт, you may have great difficulty keeping up with тchool work or bills, frequently lose thingт, and live your life in a disorganized way. Following through on promises and commitments may be a struggle and time management iт alтo often an iттue. Inattentive behaviorт are

often overlooked becauтe they're harder to identify and leтт

disruptive than hyperactive and impulsive тymptomт, so kidт

with theтe symptoms may slip through the cracks. An individual with the predominantly inattentive preтentation of ADHD may

even appear sluggish, lethargic, and slow to reтpond and proceтт information.

☐ Hyperactivity

Hyperactivity iт the тymptom most people think of when they hear the term "ADHD." Children and adults who are hyperactive have excessively high levelт of activity, which may preтent aт

phyтical and/or verbal overactivity. They may appear to be in 13

conттant motion and perpetually on the go aт if driven by a motor. They have difficulty keeping their bodieт still—moving about exceттively, тquirming, or fidgeting.

People who are hyperactive often feel restless, eтpecially if they're adultт or teens. They may talk excessively, interrupt otherт, and monopolize converтationт, not letting others talk.

It'т not unusual for an individual with hyperactive symptoms to

engage in a running commentary on the activities going on around them. Their behaviorт tend to be loud and disruptive.

Thiт difficulty regulating their own activity level often createт great problemт in тocial, тchool, and work тituationт.

☐ Impulтivity

Children and adultт who are impulтive have trouble inhibiting their behaviors and reтponтeт. They often act and тpeak before

thinking, reacting in a rapid way without conтidering conтequenceт. They may interrupt otherт, blurt out responses, and ruтh through aттignmentт or forms without carefully

reading or liттening to inтtructionт. Waiting for their turn and being patient iт extremely difficult for people who are

impulтive. They prefer speed over accuracy and so they often complete taтkт quickly but in a careleтт manner. They go full тwing into тituationт and may even place themselves in potentially risky situations without thought. Their lack of impulтe control can not only be dangerouт but it can also create тtreтт at school or work and in relationтhipт with others.

Delayed gratification or waiting for larger rewards iт very hard for an impulsive perтon.

14 ☐ Comorbɪd Conditionт

Aт many aт one-third of children with ADHD have one or more coexiтting, or comorbid, conditions. The moтт common of theтe

are behavioral problems, anxiety, depreттion, and learning and language disabilities. Adultт with ADHD тhow an even higher incidence of comorbid disorders. Theтe adults may also suffer from depression, bipolar disorder, тubтtance abuтe diтorderт, anxiety disorders, or behavioral problemт.

Chapter 2: Dos And Don'ts For Minimizing The Effect Of Adhd On Your Daily Activities

The Attention Deficit Hyperactivity Disorder (ADHD) is a condition affecting the nervous system, usually caused by the genetic or biological reasons. A common childhood disease, it may continue into the adulthood. Children find it difficult to focus on the task at hand or to paying attention to something. They fail to control their behavior and become overactive. Adults cannot manage their time and fail to organize themselves, set goals or retain their job. Relationships, self-esteem, and addiction too can become a problem for them. ADHD does affect the performance in school or at work.

The parents and teachers have a big role in managing the ADHD children. They should watch against committing the following acts that make up the strict don'ts for the ADHD patients.

Don't stop the ADHD patients from exercising: It reduces stress and spends the restless energy in children as well as adults. Exercise improves the blood flow to the brain, changes the mood for the better and makes you more alert and focused.

Don't interfere with their sleep: Sleep problems can aggravate the ADHD symptoms. So, don't do anything that will interfere with their sleep.

Stress exacerbates ADHD. Do nothing that will induce stress. Go for the relaxation techniques like yoga and deep breathing instead.

Do not try to manage the daily activities for the ADHD affected child. Let them learn to manage themselves. Evolve a system they can run.

Do not impose your ideas about life, career and achievements on the child. The affected will have some skills. Try to identify those. Let them pursue those rather than insisting on what you think would be good. Let the child take as much control of his life as possible.

Here are some more dos to follow for controlling the ADHD symptoms in yourself or your child:

Do set a routine

Routine makes the daily activities comfortable for the ADHD-affected persons. Many patients have no real understanding of a structured life. They cannot set goals, do not know what they will need to do for themselves or others and have no idea of at what time a certain process will take place. They cannot organize much. Everything is chaos for them. But a realistic and reliable routine can do them well. Begin with small, easy goals. Keep modifying their existing routine in a small way. When one such step is accepted, go for the next. Let the person know the detailed schedule and how much time each task will need so that they can decide their own pace to achieve their target.

Do use the visual cues

Keep using the visual cues because ADHD patients respond to them well. They will like and understand it better if the school time, playing hours, work period and commuting time are shown in different colors. Cultivate in them the habit of using a checklist all the time.

Do use a schedule planner

Many devices are now available to plan your day. These include a voice recorder, paper planner, talking watch or computer reminders. Use the method that the ADHD person is most comfortable with. But never overdo the routine exercise. The affected person often does not like curtailment of their sense of freedom. The routine should be used as a support, not as a restraining framework.

Do avoid stress and the urge to hurry up

ADHD affected patients should try not to hasten while performing any task. They should slow themselves down. They should stop work at the scheduled hour because they need more frequent breaks than the others. They should allow some time for an unstructured entertainment and recouping after every focused effort over a pre-determined period. They should be able to relax after their strenuous effort to concentrate. Let them cultivate the habit of meditating regularly.

Some Dos to be followed by the parents and teachers

Parents and teachers have a very hard and trying role to play in dealing with an ADHD child. They have to overcome the problems at every step. They need to adopt the following strategies to keep doing their job well for as long as it is necessary.

Do learn to stay calm and control your emotions

They must stay calm. Losing temper will prove counter-productive and make the patient angrier. Don't argue with the child as it won't produce the desired result. Be conciliatory rather than combative. They should support the person without making the person dependent on them. Theirs should only be a guiding and protective hand extended only in the times of difficulties.

Do allow some amount of freedom to the child

They should set the limits within which the ADHD child should be free to act. Don't put pressure on him or her. Allow them to do the things in their own way. Let them have some choices too. Don't be harsh on them when they break rules. Ask them what should be the consequences now. Let them know what they are doing and what they will face if they do certain things.

Do teach to avoid procrastination

ADHD patients tend to put off all their problems for the next day. They find it difficult to start work on a new task or problem. They are afraid that they will not be able to do it. Even when they start work on a particular thing, they get involved in umpteen other things on the way. Only some of them are motivated to finish the work quickly when they realize that the deadline is close-by. But, many of them panic and are overwhelmed by the sudden closeness of the deadline.

The right approach is to help these people understand why they are tempted to put the things off. If it is a huge task, teach them to divide it into smaller ones. Simplify the tasks. Encourage them to ask others how to do it. Find ways to make the job more interesting and let the affected person set the deadline. And convince them about the importance of avoiding distractions while working on a task with a deadline.

Do give an undivided attention to the child

It is always better to avoid the stimuli that tend to distract the ADHD patients so that they can focus on the activity in hand. Parents and teachers should keep the television set off and should not try to check their mails/messages or pick a newspaper/magazine when together with the ADHD patient. They should always try to follow a consistent timing in their routine activities.

Following these tips will help the child or adult suffering from ADHD to manage his or her routine activities with better ease. Over a period of time, these habits will be inculcated and slowly, an effort can be made to guide the patient to the comparatively more complex tasks or routine.

Chapter 3: Roles Of Exercise And Sleep In Adhd Treatment

EXERCISE

Your child's muscles are not the only parts of his body that can benefit from exercise. Engaging in physical activity also keeps his brain in tip-top shape. When he exercises, a change takes place in the amount as well as the combination of neurotransmitters in his brain.

One of those neurotransmitters is dopamine which affects attention. As a matter of fact, the stimulant medications given to children with ADHD in order to treat their condition are designed to raise the amount of dopamine in their brains. Since engaging in exercise also triggers the release of more dopamine in your child's brain, it makes sense that exercise has the same ADHD-benefitting effects as those provided by stimulant drugs.

As demonstrated in studies on ADHD, when children with this condition exercised, they showed better performance on attention tests. Moreover, they exhibited fewer tendencies to be impulsive, even in the absence of any stimulant medications. The researchers involved in the studies have suggested that the results are based on how exercise works on the kids' brains:

Increased blood flow to the brain – certain parts of the brains of children with ADHD are believed to receive less blood flow, particularly the brain parts that play important roles in thinking and planning, behavior, and emotions.

Improved brain and blood vessel structure – this results in the improved thinking ability of the child with ADHD.

Increased brain activity – the activity in the sections of the brain that have a significant role in attention and behavior are increased when a child with ADHD engages in exercise.

Exactly How Exercise Affects Your Child's Thinking and Behavior

The executive function, which refers to the problem solving skills set that people use in planning and organization, is one which children with ADHD find to be challenging. Lacking this important set of skills causes your child to have difficulty with remembering that he has to bring his lunch box when leaving for school or that he has yet to complete his homework.

Aside from that, there are many children with ADHD who have issues with socialization because of their behavior. And engaging in exercise, particularly becoming involved in sports, helps your child overcome both issues.

Studies have demonstrated that children who engaged in exercise were less likely to get in trouble for declining to participate in activities, name calling, inappropriate movements, blurting out inappropriate words, and other disruptive behaviors.

These benefits that can be provided by exercise to your child with ADHD means that exercising can enhance the effectiveness of your child's ADHD medications. Exercise also has the added benefit of helping your child respond to his stimulant medications if he has not previously responded to them.

Apart from all of the above benefits of exercise, your child has other reasons for engaging in it, such as:

Maintaining a healthy weight

Improving his self-esteem and self-confidence

Keeping his cholesterol and blood pressure levels stabilized

Reducing his risk of diabetes

Improving his concentration

Promoting brain growth

Promoting better sleep (resulting in decreased ADHD symptoms)

Greening It

As research has shown, kids with ADHD will find it advantageous to spend some "green time" in nature. When your child plays in a place where there are plenty of trees and grass, such as in the park, his

ADHD symptoms are greatly reduced. This simple strategy for managing the symptoms of ADHD can also be used even if your family lives in the city, where you have access to natural settings besides parks.

Moving Things Along Through Sports

It would be in your child's best interest to let him find a sport that he likes and that would match his strengths. On that note, softball and other sports where lots of down-time are involved are certainly not for your child with ADHD. He would be better off participating in team sports or individual sports, such as hockey and basketball, where his body is required to be in constant motion. Martial arts training and yoga will also benefit your child, as these sports help him improve his mental control while his body is getting a good workout.

SLEEP

For anyone, lack of sleep can result in less attentiveness. But for kids with ADHD, insufficient sleep can be extremely harmful. It can cause their ability to focus to deteriorate and then keep them from doing great in school. A study has suggested that as little as half an hour more of sleep each night helps kids become more alert and behave better.

The most helpful tip for making sure your child with ADHD gets enough sleep is to have him follow a regular early bedtime. But this strategy may not be enough to solve the problem.

Apart from increasing your child's exercise levels in the daytime, the following strategies can help him get all the sleep he needs:

Establish a sleep schedule for your child. Plan it around his pre-bedtime routine, which includes brushing his teeth, taking a shower, and engaging in a relaxing ritual.

Play background noise with the aid of relaxation tapes. This is a great idea to try when your child falls asleep. You can find many different kinds of relaxation tapes that range from calming music to nature sounds. Your child may find it calming to listen to "white noise." You might consider creating your own white noise by turning on the electric fan or air purifier, or running the radio on static.

Before your child's bedtime, make sure to spend 10 minutes cuddling and bonding with him. This helps him calm down as well as make him feel loved and secure.

Rid your child's diet of all caffeine-containing foods and beverages.

Watch out for your kid's signs of sleepiness. Does he find it easy to wake up in the morning, or does he need to be dragged out of bed? Does he wake up alert and well-rested, or does he usually act out or doze off? If your child exhibits these sleepiness signs in the daytime, make the necessary changes to his sleep schedule.

Make use of blackout curtains to help eliminate light in your child's room. It also helps to keep your child from watching TV or using the computer or gadgets at least one hour before bedtime. This way, his body gets to make enough melatonin (sleep hormone).

Have your child engage in a relaxing routine before turning in for the night. An hour before his bedtime, let him play quietly or read his favorite book.

Give aromatherapy a try. If your child has trouble falling asleep, help him feel calm by using essentials oils such as chamomile, vanilla, lavender, and vanilla. You could have him pick the scent that he finds most appealing and calming, then place a few drops of the oil on a clean cotton ball, which you will slip inside his pillowcase.

Ensure that his bedroom is conducive to sleep. For your child to be able to sleep well, he needs a place that is quiet, dark, and cool. Get rid of any noises or lights that might keep him up in the night, and see to it that he is not too cold or too hot in bed.

Have a bedtime alarm in place. Your child needs a bedtime alarm as much as he needs a waking-up alarm in the morning. Doing so will help him associate his bedtime with the timer and later on, the mere sound of the bedtime alarm will cause him to feel sleepy.

Chapter 4: Does Your Child Have Adhd?

Diagnosing ADHD in a child is more complicated than many believe. Since the disorder is so commonly attributed to children today, it has been diagnosed in many cases where it was not warranted. This has created some confusion in parents who are faced with the option of having their child tested at school, taking their child to a psychiatrist for potential diagnosis, or shunning diagnosis and believing their child is normal.

There are some professionals and parents who suggest there are as many misdiagnoses of ADHD in children as there are children who legitimately suffer but have not been diagnosed. You naturally do not want your child labeled with a disorder they may not have, and you especially do not want them medicated for something they do not have.

This is why it is so important to work with a medical professional who takes the disorder seriously, believes you when you talk about the symptoms displayed by your child, and who is not quick to jump to medicating your child. A medical professional who is familiar with the disorder, used to working with children, and familiar with proper diagnosis techniques should be sought out.

You will know you have a medical professional who takes your concerns seriously when they follow a process similar to the following:

Listen to your concerns and talk with your child about potential symptoms.

Collect information from parents, teachers, and others familiar with your child.

Administer a professional assessment to see how well criteria for the disorder is met.

Consider all other disorders or issues that may cause the symptoms being displayed.

Only after taking all of these steps should your child be officially diagnosed with ADHD. Most doctors or therapists will require forms to be completed by you and the child's teacher, and there may be forms sent to others who spend a lot of time with your child as well. This information is used to assess the behaviors your child shows in daily life and the extent to which their daily life may be affected by symptoms of ADHD.

Do not allow your child to be labeled with ADHD without these forms being completed and a professional test being administered by someone you trust. A teacher's suspicion or inability to keep your child focused is not enough to properly diagnose this disorder. There is also the chance that other disorders are mixing with ADHD to cause behavior problems, and a teacher can never diagnose exactly what is happening with your child. See chapter four if you are dealing with a teacher or principal who believes your child needs medication.

Chapter 5: Living With Adhd To Be Diagnosed With Adhd.

It can often be a big upheaval to be diagnosed with ADHD as an adult. Some people may have to completely redefine themselves. Others see it as an opportunity to change, now that there finally is an explanation for all the years of day to day struggle. But despite the fact that you have found the explanation for your difficulties, there are still many battles to fight. Most who have been struggling with these difficulties throughout life, have gradually developed coping strategies. These survival strategies are not always appropriate. It can be very difficult to change these habits. Even if you are on medication, the medicine can help to give you a surplus of energy to work with, but the medicine does not change the person you have become through your childhood and adult life.

ADHD "multitasking"

One often detects stress, depression and low self-esteem in those who have been diagnosed with ADHD. They can feel inadequate, and are often reproached by people around them. They are always on alert because they are used to the fact that there is always something they have forgotten, or find themselves in situations where they have to defend themselves. They always juggle many balls, but are rarely able to catch them. While people who do not have ADHD are thinking and focusing on one thing, a person with ADHD is thinking of many things in a short time. The way the ADHD brain works, has often been compared to driving at high speed in a low gear. This extreme high brain activity leads to an overwhelming fatigue, which in turn makes it even harder to clear your mind when you have to concentrate on a task.

When having ADHD, it is also difficult to filter sensory inputs. For example, if an ADHD-diagnosed is writing an email, with a conversation going on nearby, it's hard not to also relate to the conversation. I personally can for example have a very hard time folding clothes in front of the TV, even if it's just showing a silly cartoon. I will quickly be distracted by the television, and find myself to be totally absorbed in the cartoon.

Being in a relationship

Individuals with ADHD who are in a relationship often feel criticized and bullied. They feel watched. No matter what you do, it's never good enough. Since it is often the party without ADHD who have the best overview, it is often the case that they assume the greatest responsibility in the family. This can result in incorrect skewing of the relationship, reminiscent of a "parent to child relationship". One might start to feel that one is not respected as an adult. This in turn can lead to you distancing yourself from your partner and conflicts begin to grow. It can be difficult to be equal in a relationship where one party assumes virtually all responsibility for children, household, etc.

Becoming Parents

Becoming parents when you have ADHD, is often a major challenge for most. One's life is turned upside down. You might have formed regular routines and strategies that work for one. Suddenly appears a small child that is completely unpredictable. Nothing is as before. The child may have an overriding damaging effect on your good routines. But it need not necessarily be a bad thing to have children because children also need structure and familiarity. Therefore, it can well be turned into something positive when these two elements come together. Initially, it will be a big change, because children are very unpredictable in their first year of life. But if one sticks to the idea of structure and predictability, both the child and the parent can profit from it. It just requires that you now develop some new coping strategies, where the family is included. When you have ADHD it may well be a huge job to restructure your strategies. Therefore, it is extremely important that one's partner is involved in the process and supports the new strategies100%. It is also important that both are unrelenting. If you successfully introduce these new coping skills, children will quickly learn the rules. The child will have a secure environment with great predictability. And predictability creates security, which in turn creates well-being, both for the child and you.

Chapter 6: Treatments For Adult Add/Adhd

If after reading the previous chapters you start to think that you have adult attention deficit disorder, you need not be alarmed and scared because there are a lot of available treatments that can effectively help you overcome the disorder. Many of these treatments will not even require you to consult your family physician or to take regular medications. You need to understand that in order for you to triumph over the disorder, you must prepare yourself to make drastic changes in your lifestyle. It is therefore ideal for you to seek support from your family and friends so you can successfully implement the required changes.

1. Medication

When people start to think about treatments for attention deficit disorder, the first thing that comes to mind is Ritalin (methylphenidate) which is the most commonly prescribed medication for

ADD. Many people tend to believe that you can only treat ADD through pills or medication, but such medications will work for only some of those afflicted with the disorder. For some adults with ADD, these medications have no effect on their bodies and the symptoms persist even after regular intake.

Although these medications are known to help people with ADD to have better focus and concentration, they do not really help treat the other symptoms such as disorderliness, absentmindedness, and the propensity to procrastinate. Here are some of the things that you need to learn about ADD and medications:

* They are more effective when taken with other treatments (Those supplementary treatments will be discussed below.). You will be more successful in overcoming your attention deficit disorder if you employ the other treatments that target your problems with your emotions and behavior. You will not only have better concentration but you

will also learn different ways of coping with the symptoms of the disorder.

* Different people have different responses to ADD medications. You may have heard of some patients claiming that their condition greatly improved after having taken medications but you will also encounter some patients who claim that they did not experience any changes or improvements in their condition. The side effects from the medications can also vary from patient to patient. Some patients may have stronger immune systems than other patients so they do not really suffer the side effects while others have weaker bodies and are therefore more vulnerable. It may take you and your physician quite some time to find the medication that is most appropriate for you.

* The effects of ADD medications should be strictly observed. You will need to keep a journal where you can log your day-to-day conditions which can include but are not limited to how you feel and the things that triggered your negative feelings. Your

doctor will be able to assess whether your body is receiving or rejecting the medications that he or she prescribed. Your doctor will be able to incorporate the required changes if he or she knows how your body reacts to the medications.

2.Regular Exercise

Many mental health experts agree that regular physical exercise is the simplest and most effective strategy to lessen the signs and indications of ADD. Regular physical exercise does not only help in maintaining good mood but it can also greatly enhance your focus and motivation.

When you perform a physical exercise, your body can instantly feel the effect through the increased production of dopamine, norephinephrine, and serotonin in your brain system. All these chemicals are known to have a positive effect on mood and concentration. In fact, these brain chemicals have the same effect as Ritalin and other ADD/ADHD medications so you can enjoy the same benefits without risking the side effects.

Incorporate physical exercise into your daily activities as much as possible. You don't really need to go to the gym to fully enjoy the benefits of exercise. Even walking for thirty minutes at the park at least every other day can do wonders in treating your attention deficit disorder.

Choose a physical activity that you truly enjoy so you will have the motivation to continue doing it. Don't force yourself to run a marathon or play tennis when you really don't enjoy doing those activities. You can check out your local organizations to see if they have dance classes and other social activities that can help you be active.

3.Good Eating Habits

When you want to manage the symptoms of your attention deficit disorder, you should be more mindful of eating habits than what is actually included in your regular meals. The food-related problems faced by adults with ADD normally arise from their impulsivity and lack of meal planning. Hence, it is necessary to do the following:

* You need to watch how you prepare and eat your meals. Make the effort to spend some time to plan and shop for healthy foods.

* You need to keep a regular meal schedule so that you can eat before you are totally famished. You may not be able to control your appetite when you are very hungry. Your brain chemicals can also get imbalanced when you are starving, and this can lead to other behavioral problems.

* Always keep healthy snacks within your reach so you will not be tempted to eat unhealthy alternatives when cravings strike.

* Ensure that you include all essential nutrients into your regular diet. Such nutrients include zinc, iron, magnesium, and omega-3 fatty acids. These minerals can help you maintain a proper balance in your brain chemicals.

* Research studies also show that omega-3 is effective in improving concentration in adults suffering from attention deficit disorder.

4.Yoga and Meditation

Many of the signs and indications of attention deficit disorder discussed in the previous chapter can be alleviated through relaxation practices such as meditation and yoga. When you are able to practice these techniques regularly, you will notice significant improvements in your concentration and orderliness. You will also observe that your impulsive and anxious tendencies will be significantly diminished.

Through meditation, you will learn how to focus your mind by controlling your thoughts. The calming effect of meditation can also relax your mind and body that is constantly agitated and restless. Studies show that regular practice of meditation intensifies the level of activities in the prefrontal cortex of the brain which is responsible for our ability to control our attention and our impulses.

When you are constantly in a meditative state, your ADD symptoms will subside because you will learn how to focus your attention upon worthwhile thoughts and goals. Through meditation, you will also be able to listen to your deepest thoughts which may lead you to discover the solutions to your issues and difficulties.

People say that yoga is like meditation in action. Yoga and other similar activities such as tai chi provide the advantages you can get from exercise and from meditation. You will learn how to control your breathing and to relax your body so that you can become more focused and present. When you perform and hold the various yoga positions, you will learn how to balance your mind and body and to find stillness in your mind. When you find yourself inundated by your day-to-day responsibilities and obligations, you can always assume a yoga pose or two to restore your balance and stillness.

5.Therapy

You can also choose to seek help from professionals who have the proper training to assist you in managing the signs and symptoms of your attention deficit disorder. There are a lot of available therapies offered by reputable professionals that can help you manage your anxiety, temper, and impulsive tendencies. Other therapies focus on helping you learn how to manage your time and your finances so that you can succeed in life.

Through talk therapy, an expert can help you uncover your internal issues so that you can learn how to deal with the negative emotions that haunt you and prevent you from having an abundant and successful life.

Through marriage counseling, an expert can help you and your spouse in dealing with the problems that arise from your attention deficit disorder. You and your partner will have a venue wherein you can delve into the different problems and difficulties that you experience in your marriage which can include financial problems, irresponsible decision-making, missed commitments, and broken promises among others. A professional consultant can help you and your spouse to find positive ways on how you can deal with your ADD symptoms so you can restore your marriage and build a loving relationship.

Chapter 7: Causes Of Adhd

The main causes of ADHD in children are not due to bad parenting or even by an unhealthy diet. So, what ARE the causes of ADHD? The experts now concur that the main causes are either genetic, environmental or abnormal brain growth. Sometimes, other variables play a role too such as the well-being of the mother during pregnancy or some brain injury but these appear borderline.

One of the main causes of ADHD in children seems to be a malfunctioning of the brain chemicals called norepinephrine and dopamine which restrain our attention span and determine how long we can stay focused. These also play a part in how we perceive gratification and benefits and so are linked directly to motivation. That's why when they have been enjoying some activity ADHD children appear to do so much better, and they can hyper focus also on computer games which reveals that attention deficit can actually be improved by providing actions that are more gratifying.

The genetic link has been researched extensively and there are computations that up to 25% of individuals with ADHD really have a close relative who may also suffer with the condition. It is not unknown until the parents find they also have exactly the same trouble when their children are diagnosed that ADHD in adults is frequently undetected. It can play havoc with organizing a routine and providing a structured life for the ADHD kid although that helps.

The dietary causes of ADHD in children have already been researched, it appears, ad nausea. Actually, it now seems that when diet is enhanced, up to 5% of ADHD children may actually profit but some of the causes that are original were food allergies. Other studies revealed that there was a lack of zinc, magnesium and EFAs (essential fatty acids). There have been no conclusive studies though to demonstrate that ADHD may be actually caused by a diet that was poor but it can exacerbate symptoms. Sugar and food additives have for ages been blamed for rising hyperactivity in children but one study showed that the mothers understandings were skewed because they knew their kids had a high dose of sugar so they were expecting a hyperactive response.

Whatever the causes of ADHD in children, ADHD drugs which are psychostimulants are being smartly avoided by many parents. They not only arouse the heart but also the brain and so you will find many question marks hanging over this sort of treatment. Chances are, Attenta Ritalin and Dexedrine are household names. ADHD homeopathic treatments are actually getting well deserved respect as a valid alternative ADHD treatment without horrible side effects of the psychostimulants or any of the hazards. It's possible for you to figure out more about these treatments can really help your ADHD child to grow to be a fulfilled and successful adult.

Unfortunately, no single ADHD cause seems to match all instances. Studies have uncovered many variables regarding what causes ADHD, to brain structure, brain chemistry, from brain process, genetic predisposition, but no one can point to just one thing as the cause for ADHD. To further confuse the issue, with the launch of MRI (magnetic resonance imaging) and PET (positron emission tomography) it is suggested the cause of ADHD in children may well be brain volume that is marginally less than those without ADHD.

Since the 1940's, when ADHD was first recognized as a treatable illness, scientists have been investigating many theories regarding the cause of ADHD including food additives, food allergies, nutritional deficiencies, and environmental toxins.

2 factors appear to be especially important in the occurrence of ADHD/ADD, but not necessarily causative:

1. Otitis media (ear infections)

2. Nutritional deficiency (allergies to artificial colors flavors, additives, diet) and

Ear Diseases

A higher frequency of ear aches growing up appears to be more common in ADHD/ADD children. This doesn't appear to be a cause of ADHD but instead a condition that comes along with ADHD. As an herbal nutritional supplement has proven to work in alleviating ear aches and keeping great inner ear health the inclusion of Echinacea sp. In addition, to adding a humidifier to the kid's bedroom for night use also can aid.

Prior to birth, the decision to breast feed compared to bottle feeding may also be a positive contributing factor to ear health later on, with the position of the feeding infant, and other physical factors being the concerns that are significant.

Nutrient Want

Almost any nutritional deficiency can result in diminished brain function, with

Iron deficiency being the most common in American children.

Several clinical studies, while not identifying the cause of ADHD do signal that mental function can enhance in school going children.

Food / Preservatives Allergies

The Feingold Hypothesis is a study that suggests food allergies as the major contributing factor to causing ADHD/ADD. A diet excluding processed flour, sugars, foods with color additives and preservatives continues to prove helpful and reveals positive changes in a very short period of time, implying that the cause of ADHD is really an allergic reaction.

Treatment Choices

The frequency of ADHD / ADD has been reported to be from 4 to 20% of elementary school-age children... Clinical observations report a significantly larger number of boys than girls (10-1), and the beginning is typically by age 3, although identification isn't generally made until later when your kid is in school setting. The causes of ADHD will continue into adulthood but can be managed if treatment regimens are continued.

It is estimated now that over two million American school-going boys take the drug methylphenidate (Ritalin). It has long been associated with some quite extreme responses, especially on into adulthood and is classified as a stimulant. Ascertaining your anticipation of the treatment is vital. It's advocated that due diligence be used in determining treatment for ADHD children, particularly.

Many families are realizing that this condition is not really dangerous and that holistic, natural, homeopathic therapies are incredibly effective with ADHD children.

ADHD is a serious diagnosis. It really is important that your child be assessed for any other causes, such as mental and attention disorders, prior to starting any treatment program. Frequently anxiety and depression accompany ADHD.

There's no "one cause" of ADHD. It really is not merely environmental, economic, etc., but probably a combination of factors. Treatment for ADHD therefore should be a mixture of things: behavior therapies, natural remedies, nutritional supplements, diet change, with drugs used as a last resort. It is much better for families to move forward together with treatment rather than blaming each other.

Chapter 8: Get A Planner

Most of us with ADHD know we should keep a planner. Most don't do it, but it makes all the difference. If you don't use one, you need to get one now. Having a visible reminder of what needs to be done, is one of the most important items you can have.

It not only keeps us organized and on time. It is also a place for dumping ideas and whatever is on our brain. Which in turn, helps us focus on the important stuff. While also keeping our crazy ideas somewhere we can always go back to. Our planner really ties back into staying organized.

Being ADHD means that we have a lot going on in our head. So much so, that we can't remember important events and even daily chores. I would recommend a planner to anyone. It has been one of my most valuable assets.

Now with our smart phones, we can use a notes app. It is way more practical than carrying around a planner. We always have our phones on us. If you think you would do better with a physical planner then by all means get one.

Whatever it takes to get yourself organized is what you need to do. There is no better feeling than not being worried about forgetting a date or appointment. A planner can't forget, so there is no need to worry.

Keep Deadlines In View

There is something about the constant reminder of a deadline, staring you in the face that keeps us focused. Make a chart with all your deadlines. Or have a marker board with them written in view. Use sticky notes and stick them to your monitor or in your car.

The key here is to have them where you can see them. That in itself will help you to stay on track and not lose focus. Keeping your deadlines in view at all times make us hold ourselves accountable. We can't make excuses if we can see exactly when something has to be done.

 As long as you start the project on time, the deadline should never stress you out. If it does stress you out, having it stare you in the face. Move it close by to where you have to see it before you leave. Once again it is really up to you. Only you can decide where the best spot is for you to see your deadlines. As long as you are mindful that there is a deadline is what matters.

Don't Over-Commit

We are the worlds worst at over-committing to something. It is really an all or nothing attitude when it comes to ADHD. I have found the best way to fight this is to drop older commitments for new ones.

We always spread ourselves too thin and get overwhelmed. That in turn causes us to drop everything, and start the cycle all over again. Remember to pick your passions and only focus on what is most important. If you follow this tip, you will be more focused on fewer things. And less focused on the things that don't matter as much.

We are always coming up with new ideas and opportunities. We just have to remember that we are only one person. If you really have to pursue that new idea, let go of an older one for the time being. If you still want to do it at a later time, come back to it and try again. Just remember to take it one step at a time. Try to focus on one activity instead of 5. There is much more enjoyment when you invest into fewer things.

Fight Hyperfocus

Set an alarm clock, kitchen timer, or computer alert — or arrange for someone reliable to call you at a specified time or times. If you tend to lose yourself on eBay for hours at a time, you need this kind of help. We all have a few things that we will hyperfocus on.

It is extremely easy to do with ADHD. There is nothing wrong with being focused on something for a specific amount of time. It's when you start neglecting everything else, that it becomes a problem. Hyperfocus is one of the main reasons that I struggled for as long as I did. I would focus on one thing for sometimes weeks, and it was all I thought about. It was extremely obsessive and definitely unhealthy.

Anyone with ADHD will be able to truly relate to this. It is important to always remind yourself when you are hyperfocused on something. Being mindful and thinking sort of out of body always helps. Don't worry if you have to have someone call you. They will understand, especially if they know you well. I have been called out numerous times throughout my life about being too focused on something.

Chapter 9: High School

The period from mid adolescence to young adulthood is a critical time for individuals with dyslexia. During these years they must become increasingly responsible for their own organization, learning, and significance in life and school. Students with dyslexia must first and foremost develop the ability to identify and use their ideal learning style. Gerard is a kinesthetic, visual, and tactile learner. Staying organized and using time efficiently are also key components to achieving success in high school; examples include reminders on their cell phone and planners.

Without any obstacles, Gerard made it to high school. I think I was more scared for him than he was to be in high school around older kids. He had no problems blending in with his classmates and older students. I think playing sports helped him transition well considering majority of the kids at his school were athletic and participated in dual sports. I met with administrators and his new counselor in August. They looked at his file and we discussed his condition and the accommodations needed. Since they did not know him, they wanted to know about his behavior and medicine. I explained that he had no behavioral issues and did not take medicine for ADHD. He was granted the same accommodations that he has had since 4th grade. When school work started I noticed that he struggled in ninth grade Language Arts and Math. I communicated with his teachers to let them know my concerns about his grades. Remember we were allies for his success, so they offered to have him come to school early to attend their help sessions. Gerard knew he needed to attend those sessions, so I did not have a problem convincing him to wake up early to show up. As time went on his grades improved with the help of his teachers. I also had him review his work at home to make it fresh in his brain. Ninth grade was a successful year for him at school, in sports, and at home.

Whoa, now Gerard is moving to 10th grade. Boy where did the time go? As always, I met with administration, teachers, and counselor for my son's Section 504. In this meeting, the Assistant Principal focused on Gerard's ADHD. He mentioned that the previous teachers noted in the files that he was sometimes overstimulated, more so after lunch when he had a lot of energy. I admitted that I knew exactly what they were referring to because he can "spazz" when he is not busy and he usually has more energy after he eats lunch. The fact that he was also in this class with majority of his football team was a contributing factor. "Spazz" refers to a period when he becomes impulsive and talks fast and way too much. I encounter this when I pick him up from football practice. When he enters the car, he still has a lot of energy and he is ready to talk about the day. The Assistant Principal wanted to include ADHD in the Section 504. He wanted to accommodate Gerard's ADHD by offering extra time for him to complete work. He would also be allowed to stand up and go to the back of the classroom if he felt overstimulated in class. I was happy that he would receive the accommodations for ADHD and dyslexia. I was also glad that his teachers would understand his condition if he became overly busy or talkative in class.

His Psychoeducational test stated that he has ADHD with a combination of concentration/hyperactive impulsivity and was also lacking the ability to focus. He is non-problematic and has no behavioral issues. So it seems Gerard and I have survived pre-school, middle school, pre-teen and now he is in his mid-teenage years. I guess while raising him and continuing with life, the time sort of maximized on us. He is now driving and managing to cope more with his dyslexia and ADHD. He has learned social skills and better forms of social behavior. I am proud today as I watch him knowing that he will make a smooth transition into adulthood, being aware that I did everything I could to make this possible for him.

ADHDEarly Intervention Program

Attention Deficit Hyperactive Disorder (ADHD) is a condition that affects both children and adults and is characterized by problems with attention, impulsivity, and hyperactivity. ADHD cannot be cured; instead treatment focuses on managing the symptoms. I make chores more rewarding and appealing. If he wants to drive to his favorite store; I tell him that his room must be clean in order for him to drive. He does this with no problem because he will be rewarded with a drive.

ADHD has three subtypes:

People with inattentive type often have difficulty paying attention to detail; finishing tasks, and are easily distracted or forgetful. Inattentive ADHD involves poor concentration, where they have difficulty concentrating on things they have to look at but rather prefer listening to it. Gerard is an auditory learner who learns better when he hears information and then he can visualize it more clearly.

Those who have hyperactive impulsive type of ADHD, fidget and talk a lot more excessively or feel restless most of the time. They interrupt others or speak at inappropriate times, and have difficulty waiting their turn. Gerard interrupts his friend's conversation and even me when I am talking to friends. I have to remind him that he should only speak when spoken to.

People with combined type have a combination of inattentive and hyperactive-impulsive symptoms which culminate insocial clumsiness and learning difficulties. The approach I have found to be most successful in dealing with ADHD is to maximize Gerard's natural strengths and gifts while helping them to compensate for and cope with their weaknesses. In some ADHD children, the child is largely the impulsive type or another child can be the inattentive type, but the approach of parenting the ADHD child remains the same. The approach is to find their individual strengths and develop and encourage those strengths while providing support to help them with their challenges.

Social Clumsiness occurs when ADHD children have trouble reading social situations; they are socially 'tone deaf'. The child with ADHDappears to have an immaturity in the part of the brain responsible for social cognition and so is less able to learn socially appropriate behavior. The people who are most likely to notice are the child's contemporaries, and as a result, his peers often reject him. My son acts younger than others in his class, even though he is one of the oldest. His classmates have always called him immature. He still watches cartoon, sits in his room and draws, likes family time, is sweet to his younger brother and loves to visit grandparents. He has a few true friends in school that he can always depend on who knows him well and can tell him that he talks to much.

Identifying and knowing Gerard's strengths does not mean that I am blind to his shortcomings; as a matter of fact I make sure that he is fully aware of them and tackles them head-on. Gerard's deficits are: over-talkativeness, lack of judgment, and misinterpreting feedback. As I mentioned previously, my son's teachers and I also agree the he is overly-talkative. In class and at home, he will tone it down when asked to stop talking. In regards to lack of judgment, he talks to strangers on the street. I will ask if he knows the person that he was talking to and he will say no they just look nice and friendly. He waves and greets people when we are in the grocery store and his feelings are very hurt if that person does not respond to him.

I normally tell him that some people are not friendly and do not want to say hello. Yes, he is an extremely nice young man who has received kind words from many people. They tell me that the days when children act like him and are generous and kind are long gone. I have had people give him money as a tip when he returns their cart to the cart center or when he holds the door for them. He refuses to take the money from them. He says, he is just being himself and nice. Truly I thank God that he is the nicest boy that I know. He does not have a mean or evil part in his body.

Gerard is also not able to decipher facial expressions and body language; for example when a person is mad at him or has had enough of his jokes. I normally have to tell him that I do not want to watch anymore of his cartoon videos on YouTube simply because I have seen them at least 15 times. His youngest brother should win the 'best brother award'; he is an absolute angel with Gerard. He will sit with Gerard and watch the same video that I have watched at least 15 times without once uttering a single word of complaint. He just laughs at the video as if he has never seen it before. Gerard is one of a kind and I have definitely grown in maturity, patience, and the ability to stay calm when things seem a bit chaotic.

I was never a multi-tasker and now I pride myself on the ability to handle almost anything that he is doing or saying. At times he may throw a major curveball at me and then I become perturbed and say words that I should not say, sorry Mom and Dad. I say this to remind you that even though I am an ADHD and Dyslexic Coach, I sometimes have a hard time keeping calm when my son is in his impulsive phase. He sometimes acts before he thinks and that is sure to get him those dirty looks from me that he does not like. As an ADHD coach/consultant I am aware that his impulsivity is not under his complete control, but as a mom I feel there are certain things that he can control and he should think before he acts. However I truly know that 100% control is impossible.

With reference to the above list, Gerard has inattentive ADHD; this means that he has difficulty paying attention to detail. He is extremely quick to miss the details that are presented to him and he has to ask a few times before he can understand what is asked of him. He also has trouble finishing tasks. If I ask him to clean his room, he may begin to do it, but then he'll get sidetracked and start playing Xbox. He can get easily distracted and forgetful. There are many times when I ask him to do his household chores; he will start the chores then and a few minutes later I will check on his progress. Normally one out of five things has been completed. When I ask what happened, he usually replies that he forgot what he was supposed to be doing at the time.

Children with impulsive ways do not do so because they are ignorant. They normally know what they should and should not do. However they respond in reflexive ways to the things that happen around them. Impulsivity happens the moment that he has to sit for some time like church. Gerard's hyperactive impulsive symptoms are noticeable when he is in a place for a while. One day, we were sitting beside one another in church and I noticed his leg was pulsating or shaking up and down. I asked him if he was nervous and he said 'no'. He had not even noticed that his leg was shaking until I pointed it out to him; he was merely trying to focus on what the pastor was saying. As I mentioned earlier, the Assistant Principal of his high school said his teachers mentioned that he talks a lot after lunch and is restless. Lunch can normally tire people and make them feel like taking a short nap, but Gerard chooses to play football with his friends after lunch, so when he enters the teacher's classroom he is still pumped and energized from football.

It is not uncommon for children with impulsivity ADHD to have broken a number of bones during their childhood. For example, Gerard has had stitches in his head because he was playing football in the house with cousins and accidentally hit his head on the kitchen table. When he talks, he gets really close to my personal space. He also touches me and others a lot and sits extremely close to us when he wants to have a conversation. Since I'm his mother the closeness and touching does not bother me, but I am sure other people may have an issue with it. I have learned that children with ADHD often cannot stop themselves from touching things or people. This need to touch people even when it is not socially acceptable stems from the fact that they are seeking input from their environment in order to better communicate their thoughts and also to understand what is being communicated to them.

Chapter 10: Adhd Diet For Children

Proper diet and nutrition can make considerable difference in the lives of children diagnosed with ADHD. Dietary changes not only improve the symptoms of inattention, hyperactivity and impulsivity but also calm down the aggressive behaviour. According to studies, a high-protein, low sugar diet combined with ADHD friendly symptoms like fish oil and zinc drastically improve ADHD symptoms with absolutely no side effects.

Protein rich foods like lean beef, pork, poultry, fish, meat, cheddar, eggs, beans, nuts, soy and low-fat dairy products may be beneficial to those suffering from ADHD The best assets for helping a child meeting challenges of ADHD are positive attitude and common sense. Parents can profit from learning to taking care of themselves and managing their anxiety to manage disappointment.

It is important to accept that the child's conduct is because of a disorder and not a purposeful attempt to annoy them. Instead of looking at the whole experience in a tragic way it would be better to take it as a life lesson and look at the events positively and with a sense of humour. Parents must learn to let go of the little things, compromising in some circumstances and not have unreasonable expectations. Your child might not reach your expectations but he might be finishing a few chores correctly. Parents must also believe in the ability of their child and trust that he can succeed in life.

Tips for Parents:

Take care of yourself, eat well and work out regularly.

Discover approaches which help you in de-stressing. Be it yoga, running or an early morning walk. Feel free to get help if you feel you are too stressed to handle it any more.

Join a support group – It is not easy to deal with such challenges alone, talk to your child's therapists, advisors and instructors or join a network that helps out parents of children suffering from ADHD. These networks are a safe place to vent out your frustration and seek help from others facing the same problems. Take frequent breaks to recharge yourself.

Anticipate potentially explosive situations which might cause pitfalls - Parents should think and plan ahead and discuss an expected behaviour and routine for any problems. Kids with ADHD like consistency and if they are made to deal with surprises they behave impulsively.

Our brain uses protein-rich foods to produce neurotransmitters (chemicals used by brain cells to communicate with each other). Protein prevents surge in blood sugar which increases hyperactivity. It's good to have protein – rich foods as breakfast as it will help in producing brain awakening neurotransmitters and help the child in focusing better. Proteins should be combined with complex carbohydrates like vegetables and a few tree grown foods (counting oranges, tangerines, pears, grapefruit, fruits, and kiwi) that have high fibre content and low sugar content which would in turn help in managing ADHD symptoms better during day.

Children having ADHD should consume less amount of sugar. Basic sugars like corn syrup, nectar, sugar, items produced using white flour, white rice, and potatoes without the skins should be consumed in a lesser quantity. Our body digests simple processed carbohydrates like white bread or waffles into glucose. This causes blood sugar to rise quickly, which in turn causes the release of insulin and other hormones which cause sugar level to drop to a very low level and causes release of stress hormones. Due to which, a child may become hypoglycemic, irritable and stressed out. This can worsen the symptoms of ADHD. Suitable breakfast or lunch options could include food items having high protein, complex carbohydrates and fibre like Oatmeal and glass of milk, peanut butter on a piece of whole grain bread. Complex carbohydrates are digested slowly as protein, fibre and fat eaten together results in a gradual and sustained blood sugar release which can result in better concentration and behaviour at school.

As per various studies on ADHD and Omega-3's (essential fats important for normal brain function), regular consumption of Omega-3's found in fish, salmon, chilly water white fish , walnuts, Brazil nuts, Olive and Canola Oil leads to better symptom management. It improves the symptoms of ADHD: hyperactivity, impulsivity and concentration. Children with ADHD have lower blood levels of Omega-3's than kids without ADHD. As our body cannot produce Omega-3's it is suggested to take supplements to achieve healthy levels.

Some experts recommend taking 100% vitamin and mineral supplement everyday while some believe additional vitamin or micronutrient supplements are not necessary in people eating normal, balanced diet. There is no scientific evidence that vitamin or mineral supplements help children with ADHD. A multivitamin diet may be ok when a balanced diet isn't consumed but large doses of vitamins can be toxic and should be avoided.

Children with ADHD are known for their irregular eating habits. They might go hungry for hours and rely on binge eating later. This irregular pattern can be detrimental to child's physical and emotional health. Parents must ensure that their children eat nutritious meals at regular intervals and snack on healthy food items instead of eating junk food items or calorie laden sugary foods. TV ads which promote junk food ads should be avoided as much as possible and children should have a daily vitamin and mineral supplement.

Kids having ADHD benefit from vitamins, minerals, fibres and natural products, parents can try giving fruits or making smoothies. To ensure that your child eats regularly during school hours, school authorities can be told to remind them of eating on time. Yogurt smoothies, peanut butter banana sandwich or nuts are useful to munch on if light food needs to be consumed. Meals can be made interesting by trying out differently shaped sandwiches or serving junk in little quantity and then healthy food items.

Most eating regimens that have been advertised for ADHD include taking out nourishments thought to expand hyperactivity, for example, sugar and stimulant, and basic allergens, for example, wheat, drain and eggs. Despite the fact that studies have not demonstrated a steady connection, a few eating methodologies prescribe disposing of counterfeit sustenance additives and added substances.

If however, a certain nutrition diet isn't working for you, or results in side effects, you may need to have a go at disposing of it from your eating methodology to check whether it has any kind of effect. In any case, counsel with your specialist or dietician before beginning a constrained eating methodology. An eating methodology that takes out an excess of nourishments can be undesirable on the grounds that it may need vital vitamins and supplements.

Chapter 11: Tips For Parenting A Child

Attention deficit hyperactivity disorder (ADHD) is a typical issue found in adolescence. Indications incorporate failure to concentrate or focus, impulsivity, and/or hyperactivity.

Indications of hyperactivity include fidgeting and squirming, inability to sit still, talking continuously, difficulty with peaceful or quiet exercises.

Indications of impulsivity include impatience, difficulty waiting their turn, saying improper things, interrupting others, and acting without respect for outcomes.

Most kids hint at heedlessness, hyperactivity, and indiscretion as a feature of typical conduct and improvement. In kids with ADHD, these behaviors are more serious and continuous. Keeping in mind the end goal to be determined to have ADHD, these behaviors must hold on for six months or more, and be seen in different settings, (for example, home, school, and different places), and meddle with the kid's schoolwork or relationships.

The initial phase in figuring out whether a kid has ADHD is to converse with the kid's pediatrician about the noted behaviors and your concerns. Regularly you will be alluded to a psychological well-being professional, who has expertise in childhood disorders, for example, ADHD. There is no single test for ADHD, and the initial step is to attempt to preclude different conditions that may have comparable indications, for example, seizures, hearing or vision issues, learning handicaps, or nervousness or discouragement.

Following will help in dealing with kids with ADHD:

Think positively. An essential piece of helping a kid with ADHD to beat their difficulties is to give positive backing and support.

Numerous kids with ADHD are brilliant and innovative, and can utilize those qualities to further bolstering their good fortune. Whenever guardians, educators, and mentors find something the kid is good at, it is critical to applaud them and support those positive characteristics. Keep in mind your kid is not functioning badly intentionally and realize that your kid can learn and develop.

Characterize schedules and routines. Kids with ADHD regularly profit by all around defined calendars and schedules. Recognizing what is in store helps the youngster oversee day by day assignments. Set calendars for getting prepared for school, doing homework, and other tasks around the house so the kid can finish them in an opportune way. Time administration aptitudes and signs can help them, for example, clocks for homework or play time. Graphs and agendas can likewise be utilized to help the youngster comprehend what has been done and what assignments should be finished. As the kid completes every assignment, one can scratch them off the list.

Set clear rules and expectations. Obvious guidelines with sensible prospects are essential for kids with ADHD. Record the standards and post them in the event that this is useful. Kids with ADHD regularly react well to prizes and repercussions. Ensure your kid comprehends the tenets that are set and stick to them. At the point when the kid obeys the tenets, give positive feedback and prizes. If the tenets are not followed, there should be reasonable and predictable repercussions.

Give clear instructions. Ensure guidelines are clear. Kids with ADHD may experience issues adhering unclear solicitations. Give regulated directions for bigger chores. Stay quiet and talk plainly, and look your kid in the eye and ensure that your kid is focused on you. Ask your kid repeat guidelines back to you to ensure they are comprehended.

Orderliness, awards, and repercussions. An obvious structure of awards and repercussions assists kids with ADHD to deal with conduct. Use positive awards, for example, acclaim or benefits when the kid conducts himself well. Stay away from awards such as snacks or toys. Results for negative behavior may incorporate time-outs or expulsion from activities. Attempt to adulate your kid with ADHD even for little things. Kids with ADHD frequently hear a great deal of feedback and it is essential for them to know they can do things well. Results must be predictable and reasonable. A kid with ADHD ought to know ahead of time what the repercussions of negative behaviors are, and those results must be unsurprising and followed up on promptly. Deferred outcomes are less viable. Outcomes may incorporate time-outs, pulling back the kid from the circumstance where they are acting improperly, or limiting benefits. Each time the kid displays negative behaviors, outcomes ought to be executed.

Use time-out effectively. Time-outs are an effective source of repercussions. These can be especially valuable for more younger kids, and can expel the kid with ADHD from the circumstance that might be unpleasant or over-animating. Time outs ought to be prompt and ought to last no more in minutes than the kid's age in years (for instance, a 6-year-old ought to get a time out for no more than 6 minutes).

Overlook within reason. Regularly, kids with ADHD may cry, bother, shout, or contend for attention. Disregarding this undesirable conduct might be a powerful outcome when done reliably. Another approach to react to this attention-seeking conduct is telling the youngster in a quiet and calm tone that they will be listened to when they are quiet and calm themselves. In the event that a kid is accomplishing something where they or others could be harmed, then this ought not to be disregarded.

Create organizational aids. Kids with ADHD frequently experience issues with systematizing assignments and effects (likewise alluded to as executive functioning skills). Doing homework and performing in a classroom might be upsetting for these kids. Parents and instructors frequently discover utilizing color-coded folios and note pads for every subject alongside an agenda of homework for the day to be useful. Having a second set of reading material at home may help the kid who neglects to bring books home. Make a systematizing framework for your kid and help him pursue the same.

Wipe out distractions. Kids with ADHD can readily get to be over-invigorated and calm spaces are essential for them. There are numerous diversions at home from TVs, PCs, computer games, and kin. In the event that your kid with ADHD has a space that is free of diversion, they can finish homework assignments or different chores.

Set small, attainable goals. Set small, progressive, and feasible objectives. It is unlikely and upsetting for a kid to be relied upon to change overnight. Generally, as with getting thinner you cannot hope to lose 25 pounds overnight and require to gradually loss weight, your kid needs small strides to achieve behaviors that are imperative. In the event that you need your kid to sit still when you go out to supper, separate the feast into easily achievable portions, for example, not intruding on discussions for five minutes, then staying in sitting position for ten minutes. Offer acclaim and compensates for every objective met.

Concentrate on one or two challenging behaviors at a time. Approach it slowly and carefully while endeavoring to change difficult behaviors. Keep in mind your kid is not carrying on intentionally and changing will require some serious energy and persistence. Expecting to transform at the same time is distressing and disappointing for the kid.

Pick maybe a couple of things to change, for example, not interfering, or putting toys away, or not disputing about homework. Changes might be steady and it is essential to commend your youngster for each positive achievement along the way.

Discover areas in which the child excels or succeeds. All kids are great at something. Kids with ADHD are regularly censured for their negative behaviors, and as a result, their positive conducts and achievements are neglected. Help your kid discover what they are great at, whether it is a game, a musical instrument, a class at school, workmanship, or some other action. It does not make a difference what the distraction is, having something they can be effective at and get acclaim for will enhance self-regard.

Nutrition. Physical and passionate well-being is likewise imperative. Numerous kids with ADHD are so occupied or disordered they disregard to eat an appropriately balanced dinners. Limit sugary and junk foods, as a lot of parents discover they compound ADHD manifestations. A large portion of the drugs used to treat ADHD can bring about diminished hunger so it is imperative to ensure your kid eats consistently. Settle on sound decisions for yourself and your kids will emulate you.

Exercise. Kids with ADHD frequently have a great deal of vitality and general activity can help them discharge their repressed vitality in sound and productive ways. Organized games can give customary activity, an anticipated schedule, and a range for your kid to get positive awards and acclaim. Exercises like martial arts or yoga can be valuable as these accentuate the mental and physical parts of action. For a few kids, exceedingly dynamic games where there is more consistent movement, for example, running track might be superior to other sports with a great deal of down time like baseball.

Sleep. Absence of sleep can make it more troublesome for kids with ADHD to concentrate. Nodding off is regularly a challenge for kids with ADHD who are oftentimes over-fortified in the first place. A planned and predictable sleep time ought to be a piece of your kid's timetable. Likewise thinking of a sleep time routine where the kid is quiet and calm before bed can help them unwind. Kids with ADHD ought to stay away from caffeine, and the TV, PC, and mobile phones ought to be switched off well before sleep time so they do not meddle with the kid's sleep.

Demonstrate your unconditional love. Like all kids, kids with ADHD need to know they have their parent's unequivocal love and backing. Regardless of the fact that you are furious or disappointed at your kid's conduct, recall to let them know you cherish them.

Deal with yourself. It can likewise be distressing and disappointing as a guardian or parental figure of a kid with ADHD. Keep in mind to deal with yourself. It can help to recall that your kid cannot control his behaviors and they are because of turmoil. Enjoy a reprieve in the event that you require one and do not be hesitant to request help. You will be a more successful parent in the event that you deal with yourself.

Chapter 12: Adhd Parenting: Dealing With Violent Outbursts

There is nothing more frightening for a parent than a violent outburst. They break glass, punch holes in walls, or verbally abuse the people around them. Although not all children with ADHD are violent, there are a few who experience extreme emotions and have difficulty keeping them under control. Sometimes violent outbursts are due to problems expressing themselves. If express their anger verbally, it is usually expressed through swearing, name calling and insults.

Keep cool

A therapist can help you work out with your child the problems that cause anger and restore peace in the family. Meanwhile, you have a way to go to avoid violent outbursts of your child. Try using the I CARE method, which stands for interrupt, cool-off, confirm, redirect and educate.

Interrupt

To intervene, you must be willing to interrupt your child's tantrum or aggressive actions. This will make the behavior arrive at a halt, and will need to handle your child with your confidence and presence. Try using a code word to call your child aside for a conversation. Point out what was wrong - ". This is the second time this week, your brother got hurt, you should play in your room until you have calmed down."

An angry child needs time to cool down before they can talk about what happened. Help your child understand that he is not punished; instead he will get time to pull himself together. Depending on what the child has done or what type of behavior they have displayed will determine how you the parent, handles it. It is important to teach them that behavior is not acceptable and that there are better ways to deal with anger. Show them what you would prefer them to do like, scream in a pillow, take 10 deep breaths, or take a timeout by themselves to "get better".

Confirm

Find out what the reason is that your child behaved the way they did and acknowledge his feelings. If your child is upset and perhaps wants to be picked up or hugged, empathize with your child, but add that hitting or yelling is not the way to deal with these feelings. Ask them once they are calm, what they can do next time to avoid the behavior but still get their feelings across.

Redirect

If your child has trouble calming, guiding him to another activity that will bend his feelings and keep him from dwelling in anger. Children with ADHD have tendency to get certain feelings and thoughts, and diversion can be easier said than done. Some parents suggest using a trampoline or a punching bag, while others successfully distracting found their children with their favorite toys.

Educate

Once your child is calm and willing to listen, educate him about the events that triggered the violent incident. Give your child examples of the choices he would have made, or ask him for ideas on how to control his anger the next time. It also helps to role play and practice appropriate responses to help your child learn healthy ways to deal with anger.

Chapter 13: Establish Clear Expectations And Easy To Follow Rules

ADHD sufferers need consistent rules that they can easily understand and follow. That being said, the whole endeavor requires the participation of the entire family. Saying one thing and doing another will definitely confuse the child so make sure that the rules apply to the entire household, and not just the child with ADHD (although you can also set separate ones for that child like when doing his assigned tasks).

Studies show that children with ADHD respond well to the system of consequences and rewards. It is important to properly convey the things that will happen to them in case they failed to obey the rules, and the things they will get in case they successfully finished the task and followed the rules.

Positive Reinforcement and Praise can Make Things Better

Praising the children with ADHD who demonstrated good behavior can help boost their confidence, and make them more willing to take on the next challenge with enthusiasm. These children receive praises once in a blue moon, and receiving one for a deed well done can make them proud. However, you should never praise them for something that is not worth praising because they might confuse it as something they should always do (even though they should not) just to get praised.

Simple Rewards and Consequences Tactics that you can Use

You can reward your child with praises, privileges, or fun activities when he did something worthwhile, but avoid giving food or toys as much as possible. You need to state the consequences in advance such as limited play time if he or she misbehaved.

Being predictable is good, but not if you are giving a reward because children with ADHD usually gets bored if the reward is always the same. Instead of motivating them, they will lose interest. You can include taking a short trip somewhere as a reward, or other exciting activities for them. Make removal of privileges as one of the consequences if they failed to comply.

Other Things you can do to Motivate the Child to do Good

Create an attention grabbing chart that includes the rewards that your child got for being good. This is a great way to motivate your child as he or she can see the progress. Visual reminders can bring a lot of positive motivation in a child.

You also need to avoid environments and situations that might trigger improper behavior. Avoid scenarios that might provoke the child to behave badly.

Most of the time, immediate rewards work better than a promise of a bigger reward if the child was able to accumulate many good deeds.

Always make a follow through whenever there is a reward or consequence to be given to the child.

Chapter 14: Strategies For Parents

Parenting is hard on a good day. When ADHD is in the mix, parenting becomes a bit more of a challenge. It isn't that rules get tossed out. Rather, getting things done with the boundaries of expectations takes on a different look. Whether you're the parent of an ADHD child, a parent who has ADHD or an adult with ADHD who also has an ADHD child, the most important thing is finding what works for your family.

Parents with ADHD

Being a parent with ADHD can be challenging. Not only are you managing the world of your growing, ever-changing little ones, you are also having to manage your own symptoms. The key to being successful is taking care of you and building a good support system.

Strategy #5: Manage Your ADHD Like It's Your Job

It is your job. You have little ones depending on you. It's important that you be in a healthy, stable and functional place. When kids come along, it's easy to put our own needs aside and focus on them. The illusion is that we are sacrificing so that they can have the best of us. But if your ADHD symptoms are impeding your functioning, they aren't getting the best of you. If you need counseling, get it. If you are on meds, take them. If you need a downtime, schedule some. It's OK to take care of you.

You want to play to your strengths. If you know you tell the best bedtime stories ever but can't remember to balance the checkbook, it's OK. You're connecting in one of the most awesome ways with your kids and maybe your partner can handle the checkbook.

Strategy #6: Build A Support System

Every parent, ADHD or not, needs support. There is no shame in taking a break, asking for help, time to grocery shop alone, time to get your nails done...whatever support looks like that day. How do you get support? The key is asking for it and then accepting it (that's the hard part.)

- Take A Break

You can love your child to infinity and beyond but sometimes, you just need a break. Stress can wreak havoc on ADHD symptoms so taking a needed break is good self-care. A break might be lunch with an old friend. A date night with your partner. Going to the grocery alone. Find a reliable, trustworthy sitter. It's a necessity and will make it easier to take those breaks when you need them.

- Make Connections

Connect with other parents (ADHD or not). You can learn from each other. Be careful to not compare yourself to them. Each family is unique and what works for one doesn't work as well for another.

Connect with your partner. It's easy to get distracted by the day-to-day schedule.

Maintaining that connection with your partner, your teammate in this parenting adventure, is important.

Parents With ADHD Children

The key to parenting an ADHD child is first and foremost remaining calm. They tend to get overstimulated easily and have a difficult time with frustration or failure. They can escalate quickly and it can be challenging for parents to enforce the rules. The answer to that is structure without pressure that encourages kids to make wise choices.

Strategy 7: Establish Structure

Structure is having clear and reasonable rules and a reasonable routine. Structure reduces disorganization and distractibility by having a consistent set of expectations. In behavior management, consistency is key. Kids know what to expect and when to expect it.

- Set reasonable rules, rewards and consequences

Kids learn by trial and error. It's important for them to know they can make a mistake and come back and try again. If rules and consequences are so unreasonable, impractical or not age-appropriate, then they are not effective. For example, how many of us had parents who said we'd be grounded until we were 18?

- Use natural consequences

Natural consequences are consequences that happen naturally as a result of one's actions. They are among the most powerful and meaningful consequences a child can get because it occurs as a direct result of their behavior. For example, if a child chooses to not to finish his homework, he cannot watch is favorite show. The parent doesn't "take" anything.

- Use structured choices

Children learn self-control and decision-making by having opportunities to make choices. Using structured choices allow the child to choose between two options and then be responsible for his or her choice. "Do you want to do your spelling or your math first?" Using 2 good choices moves the child in the right direction, gives them an opportunity to be successful and be responsible for the choice.

Strategy 8: Find Appropriate Activities

Finding activities that are fun and age-appropriate is important for children with ADHD. Exercise has been found to help manage ADHD symptoms by boosting the brain's dopamine, norepinephrine, and serotonin levels. Activities can also help to build social skills and confidence (Block & Smith, 2016). The key is finding activities that interest them and are well-supervised. Because ADHD kids tend to be very active, activities with a physical component can be ideal.

- Sports/Recreational Activities

Almost any kind of physical activity can be beneficial. Activities that involve controlled body movements, such as dance, gymnastics and martial arts are particularly good for kids with ADHD because they require self-control.

Team sports such as soccer or basketball are good choices. They build teamwork and social skills while being physically active.

- Social Activities

Kids with ADHD may benefit from opportunities to build their social skills. Activities like art classes, music classes and other creative activities can be a great way to allow them to learn new ways of self-expression.

- Screen Time Limits

Electronics use has been linked to increased ADHD symptoms. While zero electronics use is probably not realistic for most kids these days, limiting screen time can help to manage ADHD symptoms. Interestingly, recent studies have shown that kids getting "green time" in their activities showed a reduction in ADHD symptoms after outdoor activities (Vann, 2016).

Chapter 15: Activities For Children With Adhd

Having ADHD children around means one need to comprehend the way of an ADHD tolerant. Being sitting throughout the day in the classroom resembles being sitting in a dungeon. It is reasonable to let ADHD child to let off a few steams after school is over, released them out and play.

There are a few exercises suggested for an ADHD child, which incorporates:

Formally dressed unit. E.g. Scout, Girls Guide, Red Crescent and so forth.

Joining after school curricular, for example, this will help them to concentrate, high physical incitement and in the meantime having a fabulous time. Different learning styles, consistent companion correspondence, close adult supervision and rivalry makes this movement the best time and appropriate for ADHD children.

Games

Group activities urge children with ADHD to find social ability by working in a gathering. These sorts of exercises give group contribution and profoundly physical vitality in this way making it a great focused action however ensure the games intrigue them.

Riddles and Building Blocks

By giving them a chance to investigate their capacity and creativity, this will make them more clarity of mind. The majority of ADHD children are known to love illuminating riddles and tests. This will in the meantime urge and thought process them to work things into culmination.

Swimming

Another physical action that requires high vitality smoldering. The fun, fixation and physical exertion of swimming angle will empower self-assurance and chance to exceed expectations through rivalry for ADHD children.

Craftsmanship, Dance and Music Classes

Numerous ADHD are known to be great in expressions and music in spite of their shortcoming in scholastic learning. Through craftsmanship, move and music classes, it can help the children to convey what needs be unreservedly.

Open air Activities in the Wilderness

Going for an outdoors, biking, climbing or divider climbing would be great exercises for children with ADHD. Other than giving they a chance to sweat and having a ton of fun, open air exercises, for example, this give them amiable attitude acknowledging training.

Practice and Gymnasium

Getting them for practice the recreation center or indoor at the exercise room no less than three times each week will help them stay aware of a decent sound life, oversee weight in the meantime help them dealing with their apprehension by managing blood stream to their mind.

In any case, not all exercises are reasonable in dealing with ADHD children, a few exercises may must be constrained or confined in light of the fact that they can convey hurt instead of assistance to them. Among these exercises are:

An excessive amount of TV

Examine demonstrates that sitting in front of the TV makes the cerebrum remains in a dozing condition the greater part of the circumstances hence this is not something worth being thankful for an ADHD child. Nothing picked up and learns through over the top TV viewing. Besides, by observing a lot of brutality and commercials in the TV making ADHD child inclined to hurt themselves.

Computer games

Despite the fact that it sounds fun and energizing however in truth it really diminishes the pattern cerebrum action of an ADHD child. The prosperity of the child is repaid through how well they perform in the amusement and this subsequent in them experiencing considerable difficulties off from the diversion. Attempt to restrict their time spending on computer games and if conceivable attempt to constrain their gaming companions too.

Extended periods Game

ADHD children simply don't have that sort of persistence to hold up and prevail in this sort of amusement. These sorts of diversion require exceptional attention just to make them center.

Summer Classes

Long stretch of school sessions and taking without end their occasions will exacerbate the symptom. Rather than requesting that they join summer classes, let them go for a paying occupation or summer camps are fairly a decent thought.

Nourishment consumption

Take attention to the eating methodologies of an ADHD children, rather than giving them high sugar sustenance's like pop, treats, cakes and desserts, it is ideal to give them high protein eat less like cheddar and meat to help them burst their vitality while doing physical situated exercises.

ADHD exercises that are all around arranged out will give enhanced conduct and fixation while keeping it a consistent piece of a schedule. Remember these things while considering the best exercises for ADHD children. Through a learn at Ball State University in Muncie, Indiana, Tony Mahon of the college's Human Performance Laboratory found that the pharmaceutical ADD ADHD children bring does not meddle with their ability to work out. In this way, while considering exercises to the children do ensure that they kept in mind their normal prescriptions.

Children With ADHD - Making and Keeping Friends

Making and keeping companions for children with ADHD can be a battle. Children with ADHD have a tendency to have problems with their social abilities. The problems that Predominantly Inattentive (ADHD-PI) children have are altogether different than the problems that the Hyperactive/Impulsive (ADHD-HI) children and the Combined sort (ADHD-CB) children have however all children with ADHD risk having less companions, of feeling forlorn, of having problems with self regard, and of agony emotionally in light of social aptitudes that are youthful or generally inadequate.

A review done at Mt Sinai Hospital in New York took a gander at the social ability of children with ADHD-PI and the social aptitudes of children with ADHD-C. The analysts controlled for comorbidities, for example, direct disorder and Oppositional Defiance Disorder and what they found was that both these gatherings had social aptitudes issues yet the problems that they had were, as anyone might expect, very extraordinary. This is the thing that they finished up; "Children with PI were hindered in emphaticness, while children with C were inadequate in discretion. These discoveries show that AD/HD subtypes vary in the way of their social brokenness free of comorbidity."

All children with ADHD likewise experience the ill effects of emotional development issues which influence their social abilities. While at first look no doubt the discretion issues that the Combined and Hyperactive/Impulsive subtypes have would be completely problematic to the foundation of long haul fellowships, the decisiveness issues of the Predominantly Inattentive are no less harming to the child's capacity to make and keep companions.

Overwhelmingly Inattentive children have a tendency to be modest, pulled back, and like to play all alone in the security of their own 'reality'. Numerous Predominantly Inattentive children have a tendency to have a simpler time identifying with children that are a couple of years more youthful than them as these children display a great deal to a lesser extent a threat to them than their companions do.

Children with ADHD are frequently let alone for playgroups, school factions, and social solicitations in view of their absence of social aptitudes. School can be hopeless for the child that always gets a handle on left. Numerous children loathe the scholastics of school yet anticipate school since they appreciate the social part of investing energy in the classroom with their companions. Children with ADHD, who are battling with the attention required at school and who don't draw in socially with companions in the classroom, observe life in the classroom to be sheer torment. Considering that children frequently burn through 7-8 hours at school a day, it is not shocking that such a variety of children with ADHD additionally experience the ill effects of nervousness and discouragement.

The uplifting news is that children with ADHD can be shown social aptitudes that will greatly expand their odds or making and keeping companions. Examines have demonstrated that children with ADHD who are prepared to interface fittingly socially have a higher self-regard and convey these educated abilities effectively into their youngster years and onto adulthood. CHADD, the national association for children and adults with ADHD is a decent hotspot for discovering instructors and coaches who give classes in social abilities preparing. Neighborhood sections additionally may have social aptitudes bolster bunches where children can hone what they have realized in their social abilities classes.

Children with ADHD will experience issues making and keeping companions however preparing and hone in fitting associate connection aptitudes will help them pick up the abilities they have to suitably and eagerly interface with their associates.

Chapter 16: Help For Adults Struggling With Adhd

ADHD does not occur only in children. As we already saw, it also affects adults. Normally, tasks like paying bills on time, handling family matters, and keeping up with work and social demands can be a little bit hectic but manageable to almost everyone. However, when you are an adult struggling with ADHD, these tasks become overwhelming and almost impossible.

Is it possible to turnaround the situation? The answer is a big YES. ADHD in adults is rectifiable through self-help techniques. Self-help techniques can help any adult suffering from ADHD become more organized, more productive, and take back control of life, while retaining a sense of self-worth.

Below are a couple of stated skills grownups can learn and use to eliminate the ADHD symptoms:

Practice Effective Time Management

To deal with procrastination and a lack of meeting deadlines, practice better time management. You can do this by setting out deadlines for everything including the smallest of tasks. You can set deadlines by using alarms and timers to stay on track.

To avoid procrastination, get into the habit of dealing with each item as it comes. Learn how to prioritize time sensitive tasks and write down every assignment and important task you may have.

Develop Helpful Structures

To kick out the bad habit of disorganization, first categorize your things. Know which ones are important to you and which ones should go into storage or thrown out completely. You should do this at home and in your office.

The second step is to create a daily routine of maintaining your organized life. You can do this by using a daily planner where you keep notes and lists your regular tasks, appointments, and deadlines. You can also set reminders on your smartphone to remind you about your appointments and deadlines.

Setting Up an Easy Money Management and a Good Bill Paying System

Money management requires planning, budgeting, and organization, something most adults suffering from ADHD find very challenging because the processes involve a lot of paper work, require time, and attention to detail.

As an ADHD adult, you can change this by coming up with a simple and organized system that will help you save receipts, documents, and pay bills on time. A computer is your best shot at hacking this especially with the advantage that comes from new banking features such as online banking, and automatic bill payments from your checking account. This will help you to pay your bills faster.

Get Rid Of Distractions

To rectify the problem of losing focus and being unproductive at work, get rid of distractions. First, alert your workmates you need to concentrate then apply the following methods to minimize distractions:

Write down those amazing ideas that keep on popping in your head then continue with your work. This will help your mind focus on one task and think about the pop up ideas later.

Look for an empty office where you can work without distractions

Place a "Do not disturb" sign when working or use noise-cancelling headphones.

Other Ways of Dealing with Adult ADHD

Get plenty of sleep; sufficient sleep will refresh your mind and keep you calm.

Create a supportive working environment. Create an environment with reminders, positive people, and a well-organized place.

Join ADHD support groups where you will receive education on how to deal with ADHD.

Appoint professional help such as a secretary, a bookkeeper, or a cleaner to help you stay organized.

Take regular breaks so your mind does not crash.

Practice meditation; meditation will refresh your mind and calm you down.

Chapter 17: Some Important Tips For Adults Dealing With Adhd

Many adults with ADHD think of themselves of always being weighed down with the demands of normal life. This is to say that they normally rise from their beds already feeling as though they are one step behind the daily schedule. And because of this feeling, they feel like they are constantly playing catch up for the rest of the day, only to go to bed and still feel that they did not get everything done.

When some of these tips below are put into place, that feeling of 'rushing around but nothing has been done' should not arise nearly as much.

Here are those great tips:

Not so fast

Those with ADHD can sometimes look as if they are working at hyper speed. So if this sounds like you or someone you know, slow down for a few minutes and try doing the same task in a less erratic fashion. In some cases, you have to slow down to speed up! When you slow down a little and think about the actions needed to complete the task, it will be carried out a lot smoother and with less stress.

Make the effort to look after yourself

Adults with ADHD have a tendency to put everyone first before themselves. Which means there is usually no time for themselves. The time which was available has already been used up on others. Those in this position will never be able to improve his or her situation until they save some time for themselves.

Understand Your Own Personal ADHD Symptoms

ADHD will have different effects on different people. You should know what your ADHD characteristics are and what makes them react badly. Once you have a handle on this, you can limit your exposure to those situations that will reveal your issues or you can find ways to make those issues work for you. In other words, don't work on symptoms you don't have. Use your energy to overcome the symptoms you do have.

Focus On What You're Good At

We all have something that we can do better than others. If you haven't, then I think you need to look a little deeper inwards. If you find it, use more time at getting better and better at your 'thing'. It will make you feel better about yourself and also boost your self esteem.

And if you genuinely cannot think of something you are good at, then try something you would like to be good at and aim your focus on getting better at it.

Think Positive

Yep, that old saying. If you naturally have more negative thoughts than positive thoughts, that needs to change. If you are always thinking the worst could happen, then you should start thinking 'what if the best thing happens' instead. Thinking more positive will lift you both physically and emotionally. You'll also be less stressed out.

Always Have A Plan

Planning does not come easy to everyone. But with practice, it does become easier. Try planning your day by making a list of what you would like to accomplish that day. This is simple planning which also doubles up as a structure. Those who have a plan will normally achieve far more in far less time.....and with less stress.

Challenge yourself

Every now and then, step out of your comfort zone and challenge yourself to something you would normally make you feel a little uncomfortable. It does not have to be anything extreme as sky diving (unless you really want to give it a try!). It could be eating at different restaurant, taking a train ride to somewhere new, going for a walk around the neighborhood at 2.30am in the morning or anything else. Doing things like this helps you grow and develops you as a person. You may not enjoy every experience, but there may be a few that you like. And it's always nice to find something new to do that you enjoy!

Only Work When You Need To

Try your best to stick to your standard working hours. There may be times when you are asked to work extra hours but these should only be done if you have no other choice. If you can, just say no. This is all part of having a routine which stays the same as much as it can. If you can work the standard Monday to Friday and then have the weekend off, it makes everything outside of your work a lot easier and a lot calmer.

Enjoy A Night Out

It's great if you can get out for an evening with friends or family. Even just going to the movies to watch a cheesy film with someone is a great way to switch of f and enjoy yourself for a few hours.

Take A Weekly Class

This could be an evening class to learn something new, a gym class to help you stay fit, a book club etc. It helps to have a reason to get out of the house at least once a week and do something productive. It's also a great way of meeting new people as well.

Keep a Journal

Keep a journal or a diary and write down your thoughts and experiences every day. This helps you to see your actions from a different perspective. It will also help you to notice if any worrying patterns are beginning to form.

Try and write in it every day, it will only take 10 minutes. And you don't have to worry abouot spelling or grammar as it is only for your records.

Meditation

Now I am no expert on meditation but I do know that it works for most people. There are many simple forms of meditation and it goes beyond the scope of this book. But there is plenty of free information online to get you started.

Make An Effort To Step Away From The Computer

Computers and internet are fantastic for those with ADHD. There are many of us who find ourselves still staring at a computer screen past the hour of midnight. As the computer is something that stimulates the brain, it is not best practice to be on the computer until two minutes before you get into bed. So get into the habit of switching off the computer at least two hours before you plan to get into bed. This will allow your brain to begin a natural winding down process and give you a much better nights sleep.

Chapter 18: Success Strategies And Adhd

Classroom and Study Skills

Students should focus on the following study skills.

·Organizer: Have an organizer to record daily tasks and work to be delivered in the future. For a given due date the task due should be written out and outlined in detail.

·Use color: Students should use colored highlighters and pens to differentiate the subjects, topics and categories.

·Review work: Each day, students should take 5 minutes to review each of the subjects. Review should include key concepts from the week before.

·Set learning priories for each subject: Identify 5 main ideas from each subject. Write out each key term in various colors and make a graphic organizer.

·Learning material: Student must make an extra effort to have all materials needed for taking notes and learning. For example, he or she must have extra pencils, erasers, paper, note book, ruler, calculator (if needed or allowed).

·Ask questions: Student should ask questions during class to ensure that the material covered is understood and there is no gap in their knowledge for a given subject.

·Highlight key words – Student should use different color highlighter to mark important points for understanding and later review.

·Notes: Student must take notes on all subcategories and draw pictures to illustrate key points.

·Cooperative learning: Student may make homework or study buddy to enhance his or her knowledge further on a given subject.

Language Arts

Below are a few recommendations for the student while working on the subject of language arts.

·Silent reading time: Set aside at least 15 minutes each day for reading for fun and building knowledge in any area of interest.

·Follow-along reading: Student can listen to an audio version of a book as he or she follows along with the book.

·Partner reading: read a story with a friend and complete activities together.

·Sequence of main events: Student will read the book or a story and complete a graphic diagram or organizer by ordering the key events in the right order.

Successful People in Business with ADHD

According to an article in PsychologyToday.com, people with ADHD are much more likely to start their own businesses. Listed below are a few of the successful business people:

·Richard Branson, founder of Virgin Airlines.

·John Chambers, CEO of Cisco systems

·Ingvar Kamprad, founder of IKEA stores.

·Charles Schwab, founder of Charles Schwab Corporation.

Chapter 19: Adhd And Nutrition

First of all, it's no mystery that nutrition is important in general. All growing children need balanced diets in order to be and do their best at home and at school. Across the board, healthier children will manage their emotions better and have an easier time maintaining focus. This is no less true for children who suffer from ADHD.

How can a healthy diet help children with ADHD? Most ADHD diets involve each of the three following strategies: overall nutrition, supplementation, and elimination. Overall nutrition concerns itself with focusing on those foods that are best for the brain. For example, children with ADHD can benefit from high protein diets, more complex carbohydrates (like grains and veggies), and more omega-3 fatty acids (like fish and nuts).

Supplementation involves supplementing a healthy diet with general vitamin and mineral supplements in order to increase the nutrients that a child is exposed to on a daily basis. Elimination involves exactly what it sounds like and can have the most notable effect on your child's behavior. Foods like sugar, caffeine, additives and chemicals can dramatically increase hyperactivity. I'm sure it's no surprise to hear that cutting back on candy can go a long way toward alleviating your child's symptoms.

Paying careful attention to the breakfast, lunch and the dinner menu can not only help the child but also the parents. After all, having a child with ADHD can sometimes feel like a full-time job. It's difficult to imagine when you'd ever be able to find the time to cook a healthy meal while you're busy expelling all of your energy trying to keep up with your son or daughter. At times like this, cooking large meals with lots of leftovers can be your friend. You should also consider slow-cooker recipes. They tend to be low-prep and can cook safely for hours while you're busy being a parent. Finally, explore the possibility of a no-cook meal. It may seem like a cop-out, but a bowl of whole grain cereal with some fresh fruit or on top is still better than that last minute run to a fast food joint.

When I'm cooking for Kade, I tend to avoid wheat, chemicals, additives, food dyes, and sugar. All of these can chemically affect him and sometimes result in aggression and mood swings. Foods such as organic fruits and vegetables, whole grains (such as brown rice & oats), beans, and organic eggs nourish the brain. I will also use multi-vitamin and fish oil supplements to further help Kades mind to function properly. Kade particularly enjoys eating blueberries daily. Blueberries are a powerhouse of antioxidants, which helps Kade's brain and body function more optimally, which makes this mama very happy.

Now, it's certainly true that kids love their sugar and it's nice to be able to give them something sweet once in a while. However, processed sugars like those found in candy and most cereals make Kade's mood swings spiral out of control. Some healthier alternatives include raw honey, coconut sugar, and stevia. In this way, Kade can get a sweet treat without aggravating the symptoms of his ADHD.

Nutrition goes beyond just what your child does and doesn't eat. Getting a good night's sleep is its own form of nutrition. For everyone, not just those who live with ADHD, plenty of sleep helps with the regulation of emotions and with increased focus. A poor night's sleep will have the opposite effect, making the poor sleeper grumpier and easily distracted. Therefore, it's no surprise that too little sleep will make a naturally restless child even antsier. Remember that a healthy child is a child who is better equipped to handle anything that life throws at them, including ADHD.

Chapter 20: Add And The Gift Of Resilience

Attention Deficit Disorder creates diverse tests for different people. It is not uncommon for people to struggle when trying to work, whether for a lack of attention, too many interesting distractions or something else. When you have ADD it is so much harder to overcome these factors, but there is one way that is guaranteed to help - develop the ability to be tough and determined.

Resilience is defined as 'the ability to recover from or adjust easily to changes or misfortune.' When relating this to adults with ADD, we need to adapt the description slightly to be 'an ability to adjust to adversity without difficulty, to make progress when faced with change, to overcome hold ups, challenges or disappointments.'

In order to develop as adults with ADD, we must acknowledge the inevitable - that we will be faced with problems, that we will experience disappointments and frustrations. But that said we cannot allow these to stop us.

We can take a real look at an example of how resilience applies by evaluating two adults with ADD, Julie and Sally.

Julie is a very smart woman, but does not think of herself in that way. She works in a high pressure office where people are very active, verging on hyperactive. She works as general assistant to a number of VIPs. One of those she works for often blames his mistakes on her, while another boss repeatedly calls Julie unintelligent.

She spends her evenings thinking of her failings, exhausted and distressed. As a result she feels overwhelmed. While she had once been a very positive, cheerful woman, she has now let the comments of a few people bring her down. While she wishes to look for a new job she doubts that anyone will employ her.

Sally is also a smart woman suffering from ADD. She had a difficult time at school, did not achieve very good grades, and was repeatedly told she was lazy, but she persisted. She graduated from high school and, even though her parents dissuaded her from going to college,

Understanding And Treating ADHD

she went anyway. She started in community college. When she found that she could choose her own courses of study, she did pretty well.

Sally was determined to teach high school as she wanted to provide a positive influence on the people around her - especially other kids. Her college counselor had told her that she was foolish to even think of it. The counselor had told her that '...a person like you will not be able to teach high school. You will not be able to control the children.'

Sally was disappointed for a couple of days but deep down in her heart, she knew different. She chose not to pay attention to her counselor and instead she formally requested a different career's counselor complaining that she should have a person who would provide encouragement. And she was placed with one who then reassessed her needs and was more supportive.

Sally is now teaching high school history and has been for 7 years. She has been nominated for numerous awards and has been awarded 'Best High School Teacher' twice.

Julie has lost her determination because of what has happened to her. She has allowed the negative impressions of others to change her opinions about her own worth and her ability and she no more belief in herself.

Sally, on the other hand, has retained her remarkable determination. And through it all she has believed in herself. She does not let the views or misconceptions of others' bring her down. She allows herself to reflect and to be sADDened but not for long.

Resilience in adults with ADD is all about moving ahead. If we would like to be flourishing grown ups with ADD, we cannot allow setbacks to hold us back.

Understanding And Treating ADHD

ADHD: How To Plan Your Child's Treatment Successfully

Assuming that you have already taken your child or teenager to a behavioral specialist and had their actions evaluated by an expert you should now be aware of the problems you face. But at least if you now know that you are faced with ADHD you should be on the way to developing a decent treatment plan.

Quite rightly, your child's psychologist, therapist or physician should now want to start out on a course of treatment . But what do you need to know before you agree to sign off on and agree to any specific course of action? How do you know that what they come up with is beneficial and the best option?

Here are a few propositions for you to think on. What is listed below are only our ideas, but these have been formulated after having worked with over 1,000 children, young adults and teenagers with diagnosed ADHD (attention deficit hyperactivity disorder).

1. Make use of all of your opinions. Have a detailed discussion with a physician, ideally your family doctor but do not be stonewalled by them. Any recommended course of action should be well reasoned and will differ child by child.

2. Through summer holiday we like to use "alternative" treatments such as homeopathy, manipulating diet using our suggested eating plans, and increasing the consumption of essential fatty acid supplements.

3. EEG Biofeedback training has also been found to offer excellent results and should be seen as an "alternative" healing method for ADD. The benefit of this is that if these treatments are effective (and in our experience they are almost 70% of the time) then we can keep the patient away from chemical treatments.

If the initial analysis and diagnosis is made later in a school year then we tend to suggest a medical treatment right away for almost all patients. When summer approaches we would attempt to reduce dosage of medicines and try the methods above. The reason we would use a chemical treatment is to try to 'salvage' the school year. ADHD may result in a worsening

Understanding And Treating ADHD

school performance. Since medicines tend to work quickly, the student may be able to get through and pass classes they might otherwise fail.

In Addition to this, by trying out the medicines ahead of the summer we have something to benchmark against. We can compare the results of chemical medical solutions to other less invasive treatments to be tried and tested during the summer holidays.

It is worth bearing in mind that physicians and not always open-minded when looking at alternative medicines. Doctors tend to utilize what they know - chemical medical solutions - without being willing in some cases to examine alternatives. Make sure that when you go to them you are fully versed in what you want and do not let yourself be swayed easily by their recalcitrance.

I did this myself for many years, and this is where you have got to come to a decision yourself on how best to help your child or teenager with Attention Deficit Disorder.

Chapter 21: Is Cbd Oil Legal?

The 2014 federal Farm Bill granted state governments the legal right to grow and research industrial hemp through state-regulated agriculture and pilot programs. It also classified hemp and hemp-derived products with less than 0.3 percent THC separate from marijuana cannabis.

With the passing of the 2018 Farm Bill, the growth, production, and sale of hemp and hemp-based products became federally legalized.

Both marijuana and hemp come from the same Cannabis sativa plant; the main distinguishing trait between the two is their levels of Tetrahydrocannabinol (THC). Hemp is grown to have low THC (industrial hemp has 0.3 percent and is therefore federally legal). Conversely, marijuana is bred to have higher THC concentrations and is still federally illegal.

Congress' decision in 2014 legally allowed the cultivation of industrial hemp through state-regulated agriculture departments for hemp management and research; their most recent ruling in 2018 removes industrial hemp from the federal Controlled Substance List as a Schedule I drug, and it allows for a hemp market and sales through state borders.

The approved legality of industrial hemp implemented by Congress also guarantees that products created from hemp plants – including CBD oil – are federally legal because of their nonintoxicating levels of THC. That being said, individual states can still decide if they want to allow hemp-based products to be sold within state borders.

Regarding federal law, CBD oil products from hemp containing less than 0.3 percent are legal to purchase, sell, and consume throughout the United States. Again, states can still decide if they want to support this measure based on their own laws.

BENEFIT OF CBD

Help you remain calm during stressful situations.

Think back when you were in college and you were trying to decide on a major. There are some lucky people who have always known what they were destined to do for their career — but for many, it took trial and error to arrive where they are now. Even more, are still figuring out the right trajectory. Regardless of where you happen to be on the career ladder, work-related stress is to be expected. People who are captivated and challenged by their gigs, as well as those who frequently experience the Sunday Scaries, are sometimes bogged down by a seemingly never-ending stream of deadlines and emails. Not to mention client and colleague meetings, business trips and interpersonal, in-office relationships.

However, to be productive and channel your creativity, managing stress is essential. Everyone has their moments when they feel overworked and over-booked, but your ability to priorities and work through the chaos and collect your thoughts will set you apart.

One of the most talked-about benefits of CBD oil is how it can ease your anxiety and worries in your everyday life. And this isn't limited to career-related angst. Many professionals find this essential to guide them through difficult quarters, overbearing clients and all of the annoyances in between.

CBD gummies for calm can support in calming your nerves, allowing you to focus on the task at hand. When you need to finish a project, shoot off an email or have a tricky conversation with your manager, the extra Zen will go a long way.

Help you navigate everyday stresses.

Everyday stresses come at us from every angle. The vast majority of the workforce doesn't work traditional 9 to 5 hours — we're expected to be on call and available 24/7. Families with children may have two working parents with full-time gigs, making family life that much more demanding. And though friendships are meant to help us navigate life's ups and the downs, they require accountability too. Juggling all of that maybe when the unthinkable happens: the dishwasher breaks down. Or the pipes need to be replaced. Or the handyman measured the blinds wrong and now they need to be fixed. Just when you feel as if you have everything under control, there always seems to be a wrench thrown into the mix.

For everyday stressors — from the expected to the unexpected — CBD oil can step in as your relaxation agent. Clearing your mind, settling your heart rate and giving you a tool to regain focus and control, it can help you get back on track. Much of life is unpredictable and we can't always have someone to step in and manage the details for us. Luckily, a trusted CBD oil can make the journey smoother.

Help reduce inflammation after a workout

You grew up being active or playing sports — and running around outside until your mother finally made you come in as the sun went down. Or maybe you fell in love with running — or spinning or yoga — as an adult.

And now, in an effort to maintain your health, strength and longevity, you somehow make it to a class or to the gym a few times a week. For those who want to live a balanced, energy-filled life, frequent, consistent fitness is non-negotiable.

Even though you know how important it is to get your heart rate going, there are plenty of hurdles that create a barrier to working out. From late nights in the office to hitting snooze on your morning alarm (whoops) — scheduling is sometimes, well, impossible. However, one of the most common reasons folks skip out on their visit is soreness from the day (or days) before. While this is a normal part of the recovery process, aching muscles can be painful to push through, especially when finding the motivation to prioritise fitness.

CBD oil can work wonders here since it fights against workout-induced inflammation. What's this mean? When we are active and challenge our bodies, we put strain on our muscles, creating tiny cuts in the tissue. This isn't dangerous, and rather, helps to build our strength — but that doesn't mean it's comfortable. Following an intensive, strenuous routine, CBD oil or our CBD gummies for recovery can speed up the recovery process so you can continue to meet your fitness goals.

Help you to sleep better

Think of those Saturday mornings. You know the ones: nothing on your agenda until the afternoon, breezy, comfortable just-right temperature outside. No kiddos or pets — or the garbage pick-up or your neighbours — to disrupt your slumber. Your chest heavy, your breathing relaxed, you zonked out for a solid eight hours and waking up ready to conquer the world. Or at the very least — brunch!

More than any other routine we keep up, including working out and smart food choices, our health and energy levels are directly tied to how much time we spend in dreamland. But it's not just quantity, it's the quality of sleep that matters as well. You may lay in bed for the recommended hours for our age group — but if you aren't sleeping soundly, you won't actually reap the benefits of a good night rest.

How do you know if you are sleeping effectively? Consider these questions — and answer honestly! — to determine how high you rank on slumber hygiene. How long does it take you to drift away? How many times do you wake up in the middle of the night? How do you feel when you wake up — rested or exhausted? Do you go to bed at the same time — and rise like clockwork? If you struggle with most of these, know that CBD oil helps support healthy sleep cycles.

An alternative to CBD oil or capsules is CBD gummy and melatonin designed specifically with your sleep needs in mind.

Help you fight against dry skin

In the winter, as the temperature falls outside, the dry heat skyrockets inside to keep you warm. Then spring rolls around, and all of those beautiful blooms have your nose feeling itchy. Summer may cause your skin to break out thanks to sunscreen and sweat — but for some folks, dry patches are still an issue, year-round. No matter what season gives your body's largest organ — skin! — the most trouble, maintaining moisture is essential.

Dry skin is uncomfortable and makes it more difficult to apply various products that keep us healthy and glowing.

Though many people turn to body butters, lotions or other hydrating gems, sometimes, it's not enough to reach the moisture level our pores are thirsty for. To the rescue could be CBD oil or CBD cream— since one of the benefits of this powerful topical is how it helps our skin to maintain optimal skin moisturisation. As with any new skincare product, you will want to start slow and watch how your pores react. It may take time to start seeing results — so be patient. And when in doubt, talk to a dermatologist about an ideal regimen for your unique chemical makeup.

Help your pet feel relaxed

Though Fido has historically been referenced as man's best friend — we would like to think our beloved pets are the whole family's pal. From the moment you took him or her from the animal shelter as a pup (or as an older dog!) — they stole your heart, filled up your iPhone with countless photos and of course, most of your bed.

That's why so many pet owners go above and beyond for their pets by feeding them wholesome meals, taking them to training schools and scheduling regular visits to the vet.

This means you are hyper-aware of any shifts in your pet's personality. If you notice your pet is skittish, anxious or overall, not like themselves, it is normal to worry. Much like humans, dogs will experience various ebbs and flows in their mood — all causes by a variety of factors.

During the winter, they may not get as much time outside running around, causing them to have extra energy indoors. Or in the summer, when it's scorching under the sun, they could overheat and have to retreat back to the couch.

Perhaps they are ageing and experiencing joint pain or tenderness, which while normal, is difficult to manage. Though you should definitely seek veterinary attention if you feel something extraordinary is happening under their fur, one of the benefits of CBD oil extends to your pets. In fact, it's been shown to calm their nerves and anxiety when used regularly. Test a small drop first — and then see how your four-legged friend responds.

Help your pet stay stronger for longer

Before you had a human baby — your pet your first child. They taught you what unconditional love really means — and how much joy a wagging tail can bring. Ask any pet owner and they will be quick to admit that their pets are not just the guardian of the herd — but part of the family.

As they've watched you cascade through various milestones, you have witnessed the years wearing on them, too. Though they used to run for hours around your backyard, they're slower these days.

And while they used to serve as your first alarm clock, now you have to wake them up for breakfast. Ageing is hard to see — but you can make your pet more comfortable with the use of CBD oil. Because it has been shown to support healthy hips and joints for animals, a drop of CBD oil will have them moving easier. Even if you — sadly — can't make your dog live forever, you can keep them fresh and happy by adding a bit of CBD oil to their routine.

Chapter 22: Dealing With The Symptoms Of Adhd

The person facing Attention Deficit Hyperactivity Disorder symptoms can have a tendency to attach negative feelings to various experiences in their lives on a daily basis. These emotions together with being very hyperactive are likely to become mentally and physically draining. The consequences of feeling exhausted and drained will definitely affect the quality of life for any ADHD child, teen and adult. It then becomes very important to find ways and means of positively responding to these events.

In an attempt to overcome the symptoms of ADHD many people rely exclusively on prescription medication. This approach to solving their problems may be unavoidable for those severe cases but the aftereffects of taking these drugs may be a cause for concern, triggering even more negative feelings in many ADHD children, teens and adults.

At this point it might be in your best interest to explore sustainable ways that will maintain a healthier lifestyle in the long run. Mother nature offers many natural ways of dealing with the symptoms of ADHD. Since any ADHD child, teen and adult has to face behavioral challenges on a daily basis, it means that if you really want to address this issue one would have to deal with it at the very root of one's behavior, the thoughts you attach to events.

These thoughts have their origin in the brain. Therapies that do take a more natural approach to improving one's responses to external stimuli include cognitive behavioral therapy and hypnosis. However, if rising medical costs are a worry for you, then exploring the proven benefits of meditation could just be a viable, low cost option for the majority of ADHD children, teens and adults.

Maybe you are wondering how one can possibly meditate with a hyperactive mind. The point at which the ADHD person becomes aware that there are instances in their daily life where they do positively respond to certain negative outside influences, at that point they should realize that it can be possible to control their emotions to some extent without relying exclusively on the use of prescription medication.

The moments between stimulus and response can be positively influenced by meditation thereby empowering the ADHD child, teen and adult to take control of how they choose to react.

In those moments one can link the tremendous benefits of meditation with challenging behaviors resulting from the symptoms of ADHD. Perhaps then the person facing the symptoms of ADHD will feel empowered enough to explore more of their problem solving capabilities in order to face life's many challenges.

Chapter 23: Cause And Effect

Causes of ADHD

Researches has demonstrated, convincingly, that ADHD is a disorder of the brain.

This chapter will show how we have arrived at the conviction that this complicated condition represents, at its core, an inherited biological impairment of brain development.

The majority of cases of ADHD appear to reflect abnormal brain development beginning prior to birth which later results in abnormal brain structure, incorrect transmission of messages throughout the brain, and faulty chemical functioning within the brain. One important clue into this abnormal biology is that stimulant drugs, the most effective treatment for ADHD, appear to have a normalizing effect, correcting the imbalances that are believed to produce ADHD symptoms.

How the child is treated and raised can affect the severity of his problems, but it cannot cause the problem. Certain types of childrearing may make the problem worse while certain types may make the problem better. However, no types of upbringing, even those which border on abusive, can produce ADHD in a child who is not genetically predisposed to it.

Genetics of ADHD

The fact that ADHD is genetic is not surprising. As every grandmother knows, there are inborn temperamental differences among children. Studies of the growth of children from infancy to preadolescence reveal that children differ from one another from their earliest days and that some of these differences tend to be associated with behavioral problems as the child grows up. For example, the difficulties that the ADHD child is likely to have in infancy (colic, feeding problems, sleeping problems) are probably the result of inborn temperamental differences. Moreover, it is a common observation that particular kinds of temperament tend to run in families. In some families, the children are high-strung (like fox terriers or cocker spaniels), whereas in others the children are more placid (like golden retrievers). Any temperamental characteristic is not an all-or-none trait. It is like height. There are all degrees of tallness, from the very short to the very tall. Most people who are very short or very tall do not suffer from a disease, although it may be very inconvenient to be 4' 6" or 7' 2". Similarly, most degrees of high-strungness do not cause problems unless they are excessive. At times, all children have short attention spans, are restless, and are intolerant of not getting what they want. ADHD children have these characteristics to a marked degree. They are often, in a sense, extremes of the normal, as are very short or very tall people.

Their characteristics are too much and too little of certain normal traits.

In families in which ADHD occurs, parents will frequently tell us that they had similar problems themselves when they were the age of their ADHD son or daughter.

Being aware of this similarity can be useful or harmful, depending on the circumstances. It can be an advantage when the parents remember the problems they faced and the techniques that were most helpful in dealing with them.

This may provide useful insight for helping the child. The awareness can be harmful when the parents play down the difficulties from ADHD. If the parents are unwilling to acknowledge, even to themselves, that ADHD caused them difficulty (or still does), they may minimize the problems it is causing the child. If this happens, the parents may neglect serious problems in their child that require recognition in order to be alleviated.

The Brain in ADHD

A child with ADHD has inherited brain abnormalities responsible for the disorder. Key parts of the brain appear smaller and underdeveloped for the child's age, particularly those parts shown to be responsible for ADHD symptoms.

The brain as a whole may even be slightly smaller (although this does not mean there is lowered intelligence). But it is not so much the size of these parts that is crucial, but how their cells are connected to other cells throughout the brain.

Almost all of our thinking and behavior is determined by the smooth flow of information from one place to another.

The brain is an extraordinarily complex interconnection of almost 100 billion nerve cells. In some ways, the brain is analogous to a telephone network, but with one major difference. In the telephone network, the connections are electrical and electricity passes from one wire to another by physical contact. In the brain, however, the connections are chemical.

One nerve cell releases a small amount of certain chemicals (such as the dopamine mentioned earlier), which are picked up by the second cell, causing it to "fire." These chemicals are called neurotransmitters. If there is too little of a particular neurotransmitter, the second cell will not fire because not enough of the neurotransmitter has been released by the first cell. Although the nerve cells themselves are intact, it is as if the connection were broken. There are different neurotransmitters in different portions of the brain. If the amount of one neurotransmitter is insufficient, the portion of the brain that it operates will not function correctly.

ADHD children are probably deficient in some neurotransmitters.

At birth, the normal brain is very immature and under developed but then adds neurons and grows rapidly to the point that it has too many cells. It has to reduce unnecessary neurons, so by the late teens or early twenties, the brain has mostly those neurons and interconnections found useful to function in the environment it has experienced to that point. The quality of the person's behavior over those years parallels these brain changes. As a four-year-old, he has limited attention and his neurons and connections are rapidly growing but chaotic. By age ten, his attention has improved (but is not perfect) and serious reduction in the number of neurons has begun. By age twenty, he has the focus and concentration of an adult and much of the brain organization he is likely to keep for the rest of his life.

Other Causes of ADHD

Although inherited brain abnormalities are far and away the most frequent causes of ADHD, physicians have investigated several other possible causes. These include, among others, complications during pregnancy, prematurity, and difficulty at birth, particularly with loss of oxygen, lead exposure, and a mother's use of tobacco or alcohol while pregnant. What is common across many of these is that each reflects possible damage to the developing brain, often in those areas thought to be involved in ADHD. Some experts believe that such brain trauma can mimic ADHD but will not produce the full ADHD spectrum of symptoms without most of the genes for that disorder. There are several events that are well documented to occasionally lead to hyperactivity, inattention, impulsivity, and ADHD.

As had been mentioned in the previous section, an unpredictable but clear route to ADHD is impairment of fetal development during pregnancy that results in a low birth weight infant or prematurity. A difficult and prolonged delivery, particularly one that results in brain damage to the infant, is also a risk factor. In short, anything that damages or impairs the developing brain puts the child at risk for symptoms of ADHD. Any damage to the frontal lobes of the child, the most advanced and "thinking" part of the brain, is particularly worrisome.

Toxins present another risk. Developmental neurotoxins are common in our modern environment from pesticides to the output of smokestacks, but very few clear associations have been made. However, there are a few. One possible but sporadic cause of ADHD is cigarette smoking by the mother during pregnancy. How this occurs is not understood, but cigarette smoke is a well-known danger to the developing fetus of which women should be made aware. Smoking can lead to premature delivery, which is also a risk for ADHD.

Alcohol can be a damaging toxin since ADHD occurs with an increased frequency among children born to mothers who abuse alcohol or even are alcohol dependent while pregnant. Babies born to mothers who are abusing crack cocaine and possibly other drugs during pregnancy are at a high risk to display ADHD and learning disabilities later.

Effects of ADHD

In any given child, it is impossible to say how much of his personality and behavior is due to his temperament (nature) and how much is the result of his life experience (nurture).

By the time he is six or seven, his temperament has affected his behavior, which in turn has affected others around him, and their reactions in turn have affected him. For example, an aggressive child (not necessarily an ADHD child) will have bothered others, who in turn may have gotten angry, and then punished and rejected him. The child feels rejected because he has been rejected (experience), but he has been rejected because he has been aggressive (temperament).

Furthermore, a rejected child is more likely to feel frustrated and act aggressively. Temperament and experience is like a snow-ball; they move in a vicious circle. We will soon discuss the sorts of vicious circles that ADHD children get into.

Problems with Social Behaviour

School problems were mentioned in the previous chapter and particularly how inattentiveness, distractibility, lack of stick-to-itiveness, and learning disorders (when present) interfere with academic progress despite the presence of a normal intelligence. Even if the ADHD child does not have special learning difficulties, he will have a harder time learning than his intellectual peers will. To learn, a child must be able to tolerate frustration. Some subjects are hard to understand and cannot be mastered without stick-to-itiveness. To learn, a child must pay attention. Intelligence is not enough.

If the child cannot pay attention to what is being taught, he is, for all practical purposes, not there. To learn, a child must have patience. Elementary school requires a good deal of (boring) repetition, practice, and drill. A child who cannot force himself to complete tedious, disagreeable school tasks will have trouble in mastering reading, spelling, and arithmetic. The ADHD child is highly likely, therefore, to fall behind and become an underachiever. As the child gets further behind, he will experience more frustration and criticism from teachers, parents, and fellow students. His parents will nag him for not doing his homework and he may be placed in a catch-up class or a special learning disability class. He will regard himself as stupid and may be taunted as "retard" by other children.

The problems of the ADHD child change as he becomes older and progresses into advanced grades. Entry into junior high school amplifies his problems for several reasons. First, junior high school is less structured. The ADHD child must monitor himself to be sure he goes where he is supposed to go at different times. Second, he has a number of different teachers. Because they don't know him as well as his elementary school teacher did, they are less likely to appreciate the possible strengths beneath his obvious weaknesses.

Relationship with other Children

As a result of their bossiness, their teasing, and their "play it my way or not at all" attitude, some ADHD children are more likely to be disliked by other children, and since they may not be very sensitive to the feelings of others, they may constantly do the wrong things. (This applies only to those ADHD children who are bossy—some, not all.) Even if they are not bossy, other problems associated with ADHD may interfere with their peer relations. If the child is a boy and has coordination problems, the social problem may be worse. If he is chosen eighteenth when baseball teams are chosen, he may think little of himself. If, in addition, he has a temper tantrum when he strikes out, his popularity will not go up. To be liked, he may resort to a number of maneuvers that may get him in trouble with both children and adults. He may boast, brag, lie, clown or show off. As he gets older, he may try to prove his worth by doing the most dangerous, and most self-destructive, things: stealing, climbing to the highest place, and so forth. Note how the temperamental characteristics (demandingness, hyperactivity) lead to experience (rejection) that can lead to misguided attempts to improve relationships; the resultant social complications may reinforce the low self-esteem and make social interaction even more difficult.

In his relationships with his brothers and sisters, the same temperamental problems lead to other social difficulties. All brothers and sisters are jealous of one another from time to time. The ADHD child's behavior and the reactions that it produces in his parents predictably worsen the envy and resentment between him and the other children in the family.

Relationships with Parents

The ADHD child's relationship with his parents is burdened by the difficulties encountered throughout his development.

Because of his temperamental problems, the ADHD child often tends to be unsatisfiable from infancy. The mother cannot stop his colic, cannot handle his sleep disturbances, cannot satisfy him or make him happy. As he grows older, his hyperactivity, his impulsivity, and the other behavior problems already discussed add tensions to family life.

Nothing the parents seem to do helps very much or for very long. Probably the most common parental complaint is the difficulty in disciplining the ADHD child. The child is inattentive and rapidly forgets. He is told to clean his room, but when he is half-finished (or one-tenth finished), he starts doing something else. He is told not to jump down the stairs, so he stops for a while, and then impulsively does it again. He is not totally unresponsive to discipline but he is much less responsive than non-ADHD children. If parents are very firm and very consistent, they will find that the ADHD child can be disciplined—at least to some extent. However, complete consistency is nearly impossible. If they are not firm and not consistent, they may discover that he is almost totally out of control. How he is handled will often (not always) make a large difference

The difficulty in controlling the ADHD child's impulsivity has several disturbing effects. First, the child is a disappointment to the parents. Second, the child's chronic misbehavior is likely to make the parents angry. Third, the parents may see themselves as inept and inadequate. These feelings bring further emotional complications because the parents believe they are not "supposed" to frequently feel angry toward their children. There are many emotions that people are not supposed to feel. One should not hate one's parents or one's child or envy one's sister. But such feelings do arise and, when they do, people tend to suppress them.

The Child's Feelings about Himself

Although the ADHD child sometimes feels anger in response to his parents' reactions to his behavior, he more often has other reactive feelings that are more self-destructive.

The fact that the ADHD child is rejected, criticized, and told he is exasperating, he will feel sad, unlovable, and unworthy, and think poorly of himself. His teachers are likely to say such things as "You are bright enough to do better. Why don't you try harder? ... You could do better if you cared," (adding "like your brother or sister"—if they attended the same school). He is unpopular with his peers. They choose him less for games or not at all. He is not invited to parties or sleepovers and because he is unpopular and highly reactive to teasing, he is frequently teased. His parents are usually exasperated. They continually express their annoyance, anger or disappointment with him. Even if they do not openly compare him with his brothers and sister, he can see that his parents like his siblings more. Parental self-control can diminish these feelings, but it cannot prevent them. Even though he is somewhat thick-skinned and even though people may say nothing, the child cannot help noticing how people react to him.

Our self-esteem is formed on the basis of others' response to us. We learn that we are attractive, nice or bright, depending on whether others consider us good-looking, pleasant, and intelligent. The ADHD child has a low opinion of himself. This is not neurotic - it is rational. He is failing at school, with his peers, and with his parents. He fails in all the important areas of a child's life. He feels he is dumb, lazy, disobedient, and unlikable because that is the way his world regards him ("bad and dumb.")

Chapter 24: Managing Your Time

Having and living with ADHD, you certainly often lose track of time, miss deadlines, forget appointments, perform some tasks in the wrong order, or you sometimes cannot really calculate the time you need for a particular task or project. Some people with ADHD also tend to focus too much on something they find interesting so that they cannot do anything else, resulting in some more important things not being done on time.

Make yourself aware of the passage of time

Since you have a different perception of how time passes, and you have to align with everyone else, you have to create some strategies for this as well. Now, to make yourself aware of the passage of time, you can simply wear a wrist watch and try to check time at some regular intervals. Also, when working on a task or project, before you start, give yourself a limited amount of time to finish a task and set an alarm to warn you when your time is up. If you are working on some projects that require a longer amount of time to be finished and you need to stay focused for a longer time, then you may also consider setting your alarm clock at short regular intervals to remind you of the passage of time and keep you productive.

Since people with ADHD are not very good at estimating the time needed for a particular task, it is wise to always add additional 5 to 10 minutes. Also, when you have some appointments, write down the time but make it about 10 minutes earlier so that you will be prepared and go to the appointment earlier and thus avoid being late.

Learn to make priorities

People suffering from ADHD can experience difficulties in completing projects or even simpler tasks. This is because they have problems with managing their impulsive behavior and thus they jump from one task to another. Thus, whenever you are about to start doing something, a work project or a simple everyday task, determine what is the most important part of that task and what has to be done first. After finishing this one, ask yourself what the next most important thing is and so on until you finish the task. In that way, you will break up one task into its smaller building blocks that will be pretty manageable to you.

This impulsive behavior and decisions may lead you to engage in too many projects, or make too many appointments, which may result in your feeling nervous, overwhelmed and helpless. That is exactly why you should learn how to say NO. In that sense, create a list of your priorities and everything that comes along and is not on your list should not distract you from your track.

Summary

To make yourself aware of the passage of time, wear a wrist watch and check time at regular intervals, set alarm to remind you of the passage of time and make priorities to avoid being overwhelmed by too many tasks.

Conclusion

Elimination diets and fish oil supplementation seem to be the most promising dietary interventions for a reduction in ADHD symptoms in children. However, the studies on both treatments have shortcomings, and more thorough investigations will be necessary to decide whether they are recommendable as part of ADHD treatment.

The research regarding the influence of specific food components and/or nutrients on the behavior of children with ADHD is currently limited, and can be conflicting at times. Research on children with ADHD often involves parent reports of behavior, which can be biased and/or influenced by other factors.

Registered dietitians should therefore help families and children learn what works best for their child, with regular follow up appointments to monitor the child's response to care. Behavioral management strategies can be employed with every child, regardless of whether the diet is restricted or altered to include certain food components or supplements.

Dyes and preservatives can also be found in personal care products, such as toothpaste and mouthwashes, some of which may be swallowed by young children. Again, read the labels carefully before buying any product. Crest toothpaste, for instance, contains blue dye; Colgate's Original is free of it. Clear, natural mouthwashes are a good substitute for those brightly colored varieties.

Most pediatric medicines are also artificially colored and flavored. Ask your doctor if there is an additive-free substitute that would work just as well. For over-the-counter medicines, choose Motrin or Tylenol, which come in dye-free white tablets.

Be sure to adjust the dosage for your child's age. The liquid form of the over-the-counter antihistamine Benadryl is artificially colored with red dye, but the medication also comes in clear liquid and clear liquid capsules.

Avoiding foods with artificial colors and preservatives has another big benefit: It will raise the nutritional value of your family's diet, since the "junkiest" foods on supermarket shelves tend to be you guessed it the most heavily colored and flavored.

www.ingramcontent.com/pod-product-compliance
Lightning Source LLC
Chambersburg PA
CBHW051723020426
42333CB00014B/1129